MADRAS GOVERNMENT MUSEUM

Bulletin, Vol. III. No. 3

ANTHROPOLOGY

NAYARS OF MALABAR

MADRAS GOVERNMENT MUSEUM

Bulletin, Vol. III. No. 3.

ANTHROPOLOGY

NAYARS OF MALABAR

(WITH ELEVEN PLATES)

BY

F. FAWCETT

SUPERINTENDENT OF GOVERNMENT RAILWAY POLICE, MADRAS (RETIRED); LOCAL CORRESPONDENT OF THE ANTHROPOLOGICAL INSTITUTE OF GREAT BRITAIN AND IRELAND

[*Reprinted from the Edition of 1901, with a Bibliography*]

GYAN

Published by

GYAN

Gyan Publishing House
5, Ansari Road
Daryaganj, New Delhi-110002
Phone: 011-47034999, 9811692060
E-mail: books@gyanbooks.com

Distribution Network
gyanbooks.com
India, USA, Canada, UK, Australia, France

ISBN : 978-81-212-4539-5 (HB)
First Published, Madras, 1901

2nd Impression 2020

Printed at: Gyan Press, Delhi.

Madras Government Museum
Nayars of Malabar
Author: F. Fawcett

MADRAS GOVERNMENT MUSEUM.

Bulletin, Vol. III, No. 3

ANTHROPOLOGY

NÂYARS OF MALABAR

(WITH ELEVEN PLATES)

BY

F. FAWCETT,

SUPERINTENDENT OF GOVERNMENT RAILWAY POLICE, MADRAS (RETIRED); LOCAL CORRESPONDENT OF THE ANTHROPOLOGICAL INSTITUTE OF GREAT BRITAIN AND IRELAND.

[*Reprinted from the Edition of 1901, with a Bibliography.*]

MADRAS:

PRINTED BY THE SUPERINTENDENT, GOVERNMENT PRESS.

1915.

PREFATORY NOTE.

FOR the benefit of those who have not seen the first article of this series of notes on some of the people of Malabar, I wish to repeat that it is an "attempt to describe the people as they actually are, and not as they are supposed to be in the books on Hinduism, which, for the most part, tell us of *Hinduism as it is not* in Southern India. Books have not been consulted or used anywhere, except where the fact has been notified." It is a product of original work during three years and a half spent in Malabar. My thanks are offered to the many gentlemen, natives of Malabar, who have in the kindest manner helped me—Mr. M. Krishnan (Malayalam Translator to Government), Messrs. O. Vasava Menon, C. P. Raman Menon, U. Balakrishnan Nâyar, M. Raman Menon, T. K. Gopal Panniker, T. Kannan, Achutan Nâyar, and many others. Also I have to thank Mr. Badcock of Tellicherry for assistance. The proofs have been through the hands of several Nâyars, and every precaution has been taken to ensure accuracy of facts.

[1901.] F. FAWCETT.

CONTENTS.

THE NÂYARS OF MALABAR.*

IT is likely that some of the gentle readers of this monograph are not familiar with "The Lusiad," the epic poem of Luis de Camoens, the restless soldier-poet who sailed with a detachment of the Portuguese for the West Coast of India in 1553. Voltaire, who is not given to redundant praise of anybody, styles him the Portuguese Virgil. At any rate he has written a fine epic, and from it I will quote a few lines concerning the Nâyars, with whom he came in personal contact three and-a-half centuries ago.

"Polias the labouring lower clans are named;
"By the proud *Nayres* the noble rank is claimed;
"The toils of culture and of art they scorn,
"The warrior's plumes their haughty brows adorn;
"The shining faulchion brandish'd in the right,
"Their left arm wields the target in the fight;
"Of danger scornful, ever armed they stand
"Around the king, a stern barbarian band." †

A former Governor of Bombay, Johnathan Duncan by name, who visited Malabar in 1792-3, has anticipated me in quoting some of these lines, and with regard to them he observes: "These lines . . . . . contain a good description of a Nâyar, who walks along, holding up his naked sword with the same kind of unconcern as travellers in other countries carry in their hands a cane or walking staff. I have observed others of them have it fastened to their back, the hilt being stuck in their waist band, and the blade rising up and glittering between their shoulders." ‡

The Nâyars, the Nareæ of Pilny, (Nat. Hist. VI, 21), were the swordsmen, the military caste of the west coast of India. There are some small sects or castes intervening, but broadly speaking the Nâyars rank after the Nambûtiris in Malabar, and they occupy the same position in the Native States of Cochin and Travancore.

---

* The first article of this series was in Bulletin, Vol. III, No. I, where the Nambûtiri Brahmans of Malabar were described.

† Mickle's Translation, London, 1798.

‡ Logan's "Manual of Malabar," page 137.

According to the Census Report, 1891, they numbered 377,828 in Malabar. The figures found in this useful document offer an instance of the unreliability of casual observation. The author of "A Manual of Malabar Law" describes the peoples of Malabar to some extent, and in his Introduction says: "The Nâyars constitute the major portion of the Malabar population." One hears of Malabar as the land of the Nâyars, as if its inhabitants were all Nâyars. Certainly they may be said to form the most distinguishing feature of the district; but, when we seek in the spirit of accuracy, we find the surprising fact that they number but 14·2 per cent. of its population.

The chief immediate interest attached to them lies in the fact of their being the best, that is the fullest, the most complete existing example of matriarchy, or, to be more strictly accurate, of inheritance through females. This system, obtaining at one time amongst the Celts and other races of Europe, was probably universal in the sense that it existed at some period in the life history of every race of mankind, and is now to be found here and there in the world.

That inheritance through females was once the rule in Southern India is fairly obvious. Amongst others the Maravars, who are, so far as we can surmise at present, aborigines in the sense that we know of no earlier inhabitants in the part of the peninsula occupied by them, to this day offer strong proof of this. I refer to the genuine Maravars—the Kondayan Kottai Maravars of Tinnevelly—and not to the offshoots settled in Trichinopoly and elsewhere, who have almost entirely forsaken all the customs of their fathers.* Amongst the Maravars the girl on marriage joins the sept of her husband, but she retains her own sept name, and her children are of *her* sept; not of their father's. Marriage between persons of the same sept name is prohibited; and this is regulated solely through the mothers. The tribe is endogamous; but the septs within it are exogamous. Thus, a man or a girl cannot marry any one of the same sept, having the same sept name (which is inherited through their mother), and *must* marry some one within the tribe but of a different sept to his or her own—of his father's sept or any other. Though property

---

* Most of the cigar makers of Trichinopoly are Maravars in origin. Their names — ———Naidu,————Pillay, and so on are borrowed from people of higher castes.

devolves through the men, the degrees between which marriage is prohibitive are inherited through the women.*

But the circumstance that inheritance through women was once, perhaps, the rule in Southern India cannot be accepted as of itself proof that the Nâyars are identical with the Dravidians, as the people of Southern India are commonly called. It is not yet time to say whether they are or are not. To the ordinary visitor their outward appearance, customs, habitations, mode of life generally, are very different from what he sees in the Telugu or Tamil countries; for Malabar, "the west coast," is as unlike the rest of the Presidency as Burma. The only other district of the Madras Presidency which resembles Malabar, is Ganjám, more particularly the northern part of it, where the people are almost entirely Aryan. The resemblance between these, the Uriyas of Gumsoor and thereabouts, a fine fighting stock, and the Nâyars of Malabar is very striking. It is not, perhaps, a mere coincidence that in these two furthest remote corners of the Presidency alone, the people at large are to be seen wearing umbrella hats to protect them from the sun.

The Nâyars are divided into clans, (we will call them clans for want of a better term), many of which intermingle through marriage, but some of them are endogamous. The precise number of these clans cannot be given, as it is disputed whether certain of them have a right to belong to the cognate Nâyar body. The names of the clans which have come directly under my measuring instruments are these:—

Kiriyattil.
Sûdra.
Kurup.
Nambiyâr.
Úrâli.
Nalliôden.
Viyyûr.
Akattu Chârna.
Purattu Chârna.
Vattakkâd.
Vangilôth.

Kitâvu.
Pallichan.
Muppathinâyiran.
Vîyâpâri or Râvâri.
Attikkurissi.
Mânavallan.
Vengôlan.
Adungâdi.
Adiôdi.
Âmayengolam.

This list is not in order of priority.

* An example of this custom existing in another land may be quoted here from a modern book—'The Caroline Islands,' by F. W. Christian, 1899: "Descent is traced through the mother—a custom tolerably common amongst the Oceanic races in general. Members of the same tipu or clan cannot marry." (Page 74.)

The Kurup, Nambiyâr, Viyyûr, Mânavallan, Vengôlan, Nelliôden, Adungâdi, Kitâvu, Adiôdi, Âmayengolam, all superior clans, belong, properly speaking, to North Malabar. The Kiriyattil, or Kiriyam, said to be derived from the Sanskrit graham, a house (a doubtful derivation) is the highest of all the clans in South Malabar, and is supposed to comprise or correspond with the group of clans just named of North Malabar. In the old days every Nâyar chief had his Chârnavar, or adherents. The Purattu Chârna are the *outside* adherents, or the fighters, and so on, and the Akattu Chârna are *inside* adherents—clerks and domestics. The clan from which the former were drawn is superior to the latter. The Urâli are said to have been masons; the Pallichans, mancheel* bearers.†

The Vattakkâd clan, whose proper métier is producing gingelly or cocoanut oil with the oil mill, is the lowest of all excepting, I think, the Pallichan. Indeed, in North Malabar, I have frequently been told by Nâyars of the superior clans that they do not admit the Vattakkâd to be Nâyars, and say they have adopted the honorific affix "Nâyar" to their names quite recently. It seems rather odd that this clan, or at any rate one sub-clan of it is almost the tallest and has the finest nasal index, being the only clan whose nasal index is finer than that of the Nambûtiri.

Union by marriage, or whatever the function may be called, is permissible between most of the other clans, the rule which was noticed already under "Nambûtiris"‡ by which a woman may never unite herself with her inferior, being always observed. That is, she may unite herself with a man of her own clan or with a man of any superior clan, or with a Nambûtiri, an Embrântiri or any other Brâhman, or with one of the small sects coming between the Brâhmans and the Nâyars, but she cannot under any circumstances unite herself with a man of a clan which is inferior to hers. Nor can she eat with others of a clan inferior to hers. A man may, and does without restriction. Her children, by an equal in race and not only in mere social standing, but never by one

* A mancheel is a conveyance carried on men's shoulders, more like a hammock *slung* on a pole, with a flat covering over it, than a palankeen. The palankeen is unknown in Malabar.

† There is in the Cochin state a clan, Elâyadan, which is practically equal in status to the Nambûtiri.

‡ Madras Government Museum Bulletin, Vol. III, No. 1.

who is racially inferior, belong to *her* Taravâd. The children of the inferior mothers are never brought into the Taravâd of the superior fathers. That is, they are never brought into it to *belong* to it. But they may live there. And where they do so, they cannot enter the Taravâd kitchen or touch the women while they are eating. Nor are they allowed to touch their father's corpse. They may live in the Taravâd, under these and other disabilities, but they are never *of* it.

It will be as well to avoid here a possible error that may have arisen from the statement that most of the clans may intermingle. Those of the same clan name may marry. The Nâyars of North Malabar are held to be superior all along the line, clan for clan, to those of South Malabar, which is divided from the north by the river Korapuzha, 7 miles north of Calicut; so that a woman of North Malabar would not unite herself to a man of her own clan name of South Malabar. There will be more to say on the point when we come to "Marriage." A Nâyar woman of North Malabar cannot pass northward beyond the frontier; she cannot pass the hills to the eastward; and she cannot cross the Korapuzha to the south. It is tabu. To the west is the sea. The women of South Malabar are similarly confined by *custom*, breach of which involves forfeiture of caste. To this rule there is what appears to be an exception, and this exception is now having some slight effect, since of late years the world has come in touch with the Malayâli who now-a-days goes to the University, studies medicine and law in the Presidency town or even in far off England. It is that women of the relatively inferior Akattu Chârna clan are not under quite the same restrictions as regards residence as are those of most of the other clans; so in these days of free communications when Malayâlis travel and frequently reside far from their own country, they often prefer to select wives from this Akatta Chârna clan. This may have some effect on the status of the clan.

But the old order changeth everywhere, and now-a-days Malayâlis who are in the Government service and obliged to reside far away from Malabar, and a few who have taken up their abode in the Presidency town, have wrenched themselves free of the bonds of custom, and taken with them their wives who are of clans other than the Akatta Chârna. But this is more new fangled than orthodox. The interdiction to travel, and the possible exception to it in the case of the Akattu Chârna women, has been explained to me in this way. The Nâyar woman observes pollution for three days during menstruation. While in her period she may not eat or drink with any other member of the Taravâd, and at the end of it, that is on the fourth day, she must be purified. Purification is known as "mâttu" (change), and it is effected by the washerwoman who, in some parts of South Malabar, is of the *Mannan* or Vannan caste (whose *métier* it is to wash for the Nâyars and Nambûtiris), but who is, as a rule, the washerwoman of the Tîyan caste, giving her, after her bath, *one of her own* clean cloths to wear (which is called mattu, change of raiment) instead of the soiled cloth which she takes away to wash. Pollution, which may come through a death in the family, through child birth, or menstruation *must* be removed by "mâttu." There is no avoiding it.* Until it is done, and it *must* be done on the fourth day, the woman is out of caste. It must be done in the right way at the right moment under pain of the most unpleasant social consequences. How that the influential rural local magnate wreaks vengeance on a Taravâd by preventing the right person giving "mâttu" to the women is well known in Malabar. He could not with all the sections of the Penal Code at his disposal inflict deeper injury. Now the Nâyar woman is said to feel compelled to remain in Malabar, or within her own part of it, in order to be within reach of "mâttu." My informant here tells me that the Vannan caste being peculiar to Malabar, the Nâyar women cannot go where these are not to be found; and that "mâttu" must be done by one of that caste. But this is not the rule. I know from my own observation in the most truly conservative localities, in Kurumbranâd for instance, where the Nâyar has a relative superiority, that the washerman is as a rule a Tîyan; and I cannot but think that the interdiction has other roots than those involved in "mâttu." It does not account for the superstition against crossing water which has its counterparts elsewhere in the world. As bearing on this point I may mention that the Nâyar women living to the east of Calicut cannot cross the river-backwater and come into the town.

The Zamorin is the over-lord of the Akattu Chârna clan, and with the decline of his power and influence, it may be that the women of it have latterly taken more liberty than was formerly possible.

---

* More will be said on this point when we come to describe the Tîyans.

The Sûdra clan, one of the best, supplies the women servants in the Nambûtiris' houses.

We will now pass to a consideration of the physical measures of some of the clans—men, not women unfortunately. It was impossible to measure the women.

Here are given the averages of the various measures of 186 Nâyars—

25 Kiriattil.	25 Vattakkâd.
25 Úrâli.	25 Purattu Chârna.
8 Kurup.	25 Akattu Chârna.
22 Nambiyâr.	25 Sûdra.

Note.—Group A, a non-descript group of a few individuals of eight different clans (see "Nambûtiris"—Bulletin, Vol. III, No. I, page 10) is not included here for obvious reasons.

Each index given is the mean of the indices—

	Average of 186 Nâyars.
Stature	165·6
Height, sitting	84·9
Do. kneeling	122·4
Span	175·1
Chest	80·6
Shoulders	40·0
Left cubit	46·2
Left hand, length	18·5
Do. width	8·3
Left middle finger	11·0
Hips	26·0
Left foot, length	25·4
Do. width	8·8
Cephalic length	19·2
Do. width	14·1
Do. index	73·1
Bigoniac	10·4
Bizygomatic	13·1
Maxillo-zygomatic index	80·1
Nasal height	4·8
Do. width	3·6
Do. index	76·8
Vertex to tragus	13·1
Do. to chin	19·7
Middle finger to patella	10·1

The physical characteristics of each clan separately will be given first. This table will enable us to see at a glance how the measures of any particular clan differ from those of the average Nâyar ; also how the averages compare with the Nambûtiri.

But, before doing this, we will exclude the endogamous clans—the Ùrâli (wholly endogamous) and the Vattakkâd (partly endogamous), and take the averages of all the others. It will be observed that exclusion of these two, who are each units apart from each other, and the first from all the others here dealt with, leaves the averages of all those who intermingle much the same as before, when the Ùrâli and Vattakkâd were included. It cannot be said that exclusion of these two bring the measures of the others any nearer to those of the Nambûtiri, whose blood is in constant process of mixture with the others, but not at all with the Úrâli and not much with the Vattakkâd. It must, however, be remembered that there are about 39 Nâyars to every Nambûtiri in Malabar, and that the latter does not waive his opportunities to disperse his favours amongst the Nâyar ladies.

The Úrâli and the Vattakkâd are not the only clans wholly or partly endogamous, but they are the only clans wholly or partly endogamous which have been examined thoroughly by me. The Attikkurissi clan is also endogamous, and there may be others.

Note.—Individuals in the constabulary are excluded from all the tables, their measures being as a matter of course above the averages for their caste or clan.

	Averages of 136 Nâyars, Vattakkâd and Úrâli excluded.
Stature	165·7
Height, sitting	85·1
Do. kneeling	122·7
Span	175·3
Chest	80·4
Shoulders	40·0
Left cubit	46·2
Left hand, length	18·6
Do. width	8·0
Left middle finger...	10·9
Hips	25·9
Left foot, length	25·5
Do. width	8·8
Cephalic length	19·3
Do. width	14·1
Do. index	72·9

	Average of 136 Nâyars, Vattakkâd and Ûrâli excluded.
Bigoniac	10·4
Bizygomatic	13·0
Maxillo-zygomatic index	80·0
Nasal height	4·8
Do. width	3·7
Do. index	77·6
Vertex to tragus	13·1
Do. to chin	19·7
Middle finger to patella	10·0

KIRIATTIL NÂYARS.

Ages ranging between 22 and 52.	Maximum.	Minimum.	Average of 25.	To stature = 100.	Remarks.
Stature, height ...	175·2	155 1	165·3	...	
Height, sitting ...	89·7	80·4	84·3	51·0	
Do. kneeling ...	129·5	113·8	122·0	73·8	
Span	186·0	160·4	174·3	105·4	
Chest	87·6	75·0	78·2	47·3	
Shoulders	42·8	37·7	39·4	23·8	
Left cubit	47·8	42·7	45·9	27·8	
Left hand, length ...	19·5	16·6	18·3	11·1	
Do. width ...	8·6	7·6	8·2	44·3	To left hand, length = 100.
Left middle finger ...	11·5	9·1	10·7	57·8	To left hand, length = 100.
Hips	27·9	24·4	26·0	15·7	
Left foot, length ...	26·8	23·2	25·3	15·3	
Do. width ...	9·8	8·0	8·8	13·9	
Cephalic length ...	20·1	17·5	19·0	11·5	
Do. width ...	14·6	13·3	13·9	...	
Do. index ...	80·0	69·0	73·1	...	
Bigoniac	11·3	9·1	10·4	...	
Bizygomatic ...	14·1	12·2	13·0	...	
Maxillo-zygomatic index.	84·8	73·4	80·1	...	
Nasal height ...	5·1	4·2	4·7	...	There are 8 whose nasal height is 5 and over.
Do. width	4·4	3·2	3·7	...	
Do. index	102·3	66·7	78·8	...	
Vertex to tragus ...	14·4	12·0	12·9	7·8	
Do. to chin ...	20·8	17·5	19·2	11·6	
Middle finger to patella.	14·7	5·5	9·7	5·86	

Face.—Supraciliary arches prominent in two. Face of one distinctly pyramidal; in two others it was rather so.

In one the broadest part of the head was immediately behind the ears, low down.

Figure.—Fifteen are noted slight, four as slight to medium, five as medium. Two were marked as powerfully built.

Hair.—An oval patch of hair on the vertex remains; the rest of the head, the face and body are always shaved. A moustache is never worn. The men are always clean shaven except during mourning for a near relative, when the razor is not used for a year. The hair on the vertex is allowed to grow long, and well treated with oil, looks glossy and black, is tied in a knot which hangs over the forehead or to one side of the head at the pleasure of the wearer. As a rule the hair on the head is plentiful and wavy, while in a few it is very thick. About 20 per cent. of those examined had scanty hair on the head. The following facts were recorded:—

A man of 50 had a few gray hairs.

A man of 49 had hair distinctly gray: on the face, white when sprouting.

A man of 52 had a few white hairs on the sternum; not on the head.

Baldness is uncommon; and, though old age does not overtake them too early, it has been noted that one man of 40 looked about 60.

Gingelly oil is commonly used for the hair, but its use for the hair is said by some to have certain effects on the body. One man said he used cocoanut oil because, if he used the other, he would get boils all over his body and suffer from headaches. It is usual to oil the head profusely during the month Karkadagam * "in order to cool the body."

Hair on the chest and arms.—As a rule the growth is slight to very slight in 14 out of 25, while in the remaining 11 it is moderate.

On the legs.—In 20 per cent. it was slight; in the rest moderate or thick.

Note.—Men never shave themselves. With the exception of the oval patch on the crown of the head, about 7½ inches long and 5½ inches wide where the hair is allowed to grow long, all hair on the head, face, chest, abdomen, armpits, wrists and about the pubes is shaved by the barber. The back is not shaved, nor the legs: the arms sometimes, but not always. A few do not shave the chest.

* During the rains.

Nâyar women of all classes shave the hair about the vagina. They shave themselves, standing, placing one foot on a bench or anything a couple of feet or so from the ground, thus raising the leg. The use of scissors for this purpose is rare, new fangled and not sanctified by custom. In a few houses now-a-days razors of English or German manufacture are kept for the use of the women; but according to general custom the barber woman pays periodical visits, and the women of the house receive from her a razor, with which they shave themselves. The armpits, the eyebrows and stray hairs on any other part of the body, excepting of course the head, are shaved by the barber woman. I have it an excellent authority that some of the elderly women—possibly those who are old and fleshy—submit their entire person to the barber woman's razor. The young women never.

In the Tamil country the women, as is well known, use a depilatory. Possibly the Nâyar women resort to shaving in order to avoid the unpleasant odour of the depilatory. The reason for shaving or destroying the hair on that part of the body is not apparent. No reason is assigned for it. Very likely the custom arose out of necessities for cleanliness, when the Nâyars were not the clean people they are now, and like all customs has persisted aimlessly.

Colour of the skin.—Using Broca's colour tables. The darkest was as No. 43 (one only); the fairest, 44 to 30. Two others were fair or very nearly so. The colour number for 5 was 37; for 5 was 28; for 13 was 29, and lighter. Darker than the Nambûtiri. The women, who are not so much exposed to the sun, are distinctly fair as well as well favoured. Many are very handsome.

Colour of the eyes.—Out of 20 individuals (using Broca's colour tables for the eyes), in 13 the number corresponding to their eyes was 2, while in 7 it was 1 to a little lighter. So that the eye is, as a rule, brown; rarely black.

Ornaments, men.—Not much jewellery is worn. One or two golden earrings called kadukkans are worn, as a rule, in each ear by those who can afford to do so. Some of the members of this clan who call themselves "Paḍi-nâyirattil"—"one of 10,000"—doubtless a relic of the old Nâyar military system, pierce the ears, but never wear earrings. The title of the hereditary chief of these is Ayyâyira Prabhu Karttâvu. The 10,000 do not, however, all belong to this clan. I came across a man of the Nambiyâr clan who belonged to it, and he too could not wear earrings. Rings and amulets are also worn commonly.

One individual wore 2 golden earrings, of the pattern called kadukkan in each ear.

One individual wore two rings made of an amalgam of gold and copper, called "tambâk" in the vernacular, on the ring finger of the right hand, for good luck. "Tambâk" rings are lucky rings. It is a good thing to wash the face with the hand on which is a "tambâk" ring. I see in my notes a record of an individual who wore one of these rings on the second finger of the left hand. They are common.

One individual wore two rings of the pattern called triloham (lit: metals) on the ring finger of each hand. Each of these rings was made during an eclipse!

One individual wore a silver bangle as a vow. It was to be given up at the next festival to be held at a place called Kottiôre, a famous festival in North Malabar, the scene of it being far away in the forest under the hills. He also wore a "tambâk" ring on the ring finger of the right hand for luck; and a thin iron ring on the ring finger of the left hand.

One individual wore no jewellery, but there was a small circular tattooed spot in the centre of the forehead over the glabella. Tattooing is not common. This individual is the only one of those examined who was tattooed.

Women.—The style of the jewellery worn by the women will be seen in the *plate.* It is altogether unlike any other South Indian jewellery. The necklaces are almost identical in form, shape and general character with those of Sindh. Silver is never worn.

The lobes of the ears are dilated in childhood generally in the sixth month and in them are worn large spiral rings of white metal or the more solid "tôda," really a handsome ornament, in the groove of which the elongated ear-lobe is almost concealed. It is made of gold. Properly speaking the tôda is an ornament worn exclusively by the Nâyar women. Several necklaces are often worn at the same time. The Venetian sequin, which probably first found its way hither in the days of Vasco da Gama and Albuquerque, is one of those coins which, having found favour with a people, is used persistently in ornamentation long after it has passed out of currency; thus illustrating the well-known thesis that things originally made for use, by and by pass into ornament. There are instances of this use of coins in Europe, of course, as amongst the Swabian peasantry. So fond are the Malayalis—those of Malabar, Cochin and Travancore—of the sequin that to this day there is quite a large trade in imitations of the coin for purposes of ornament. Such is the persistence of its use that the trade extends to brass and even copper imitations of the sequin. The former, brought from Europe, are often seen to bear the

PL. VII.

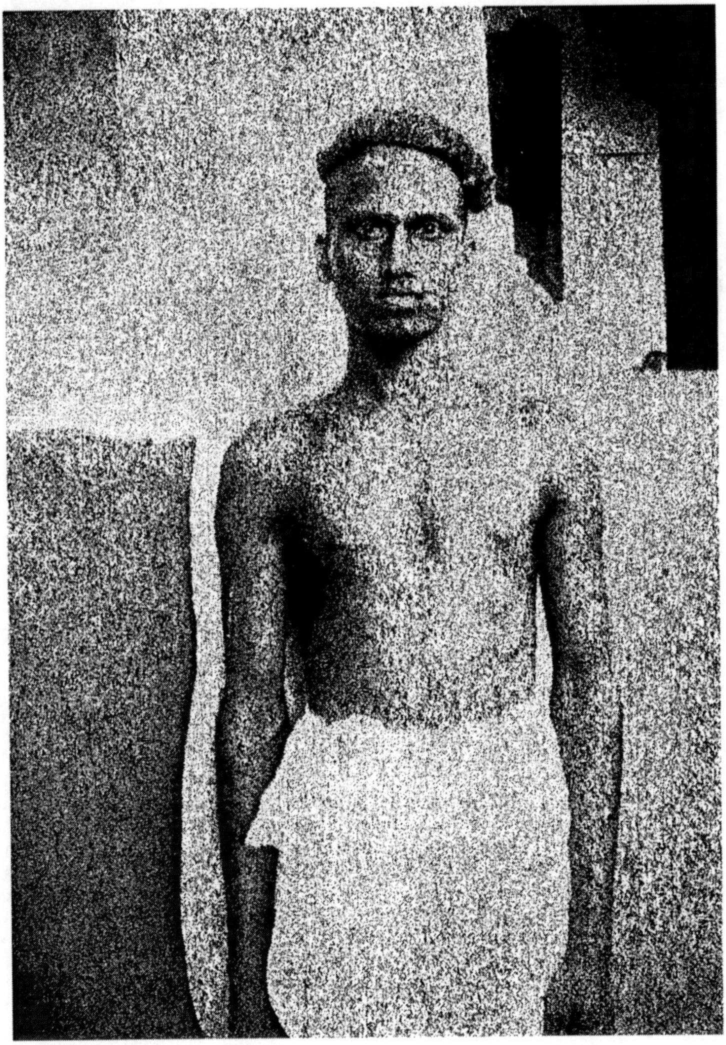

AKATTU CHARNA NAYAR. FATHER A NAMBUTIRI.

legend "made in Austria." The Nâyars wear none but the gold, "mounted" as they call it (the mounting being much as the upper portion of one section of the necklace, in the plate), strung together through the mounting just as the necklace: a very effective ornament for the neck. The brass imitations of the sequin are worn by the women of the inferior races of whom we shall have some description hereafter. If one asks the ordinary Malayali, say a Nâyar, what persons are represented on the sequin, one gets for answer that they are Rama and Sita; between them a cocoanut tree!

Turkish coins, French half louis, and German 10 mark pieces are also used in the same way, each one being known by a distinctive vernacular name, and no corruption of its nomenclature in European coinage, so that it is always easy to identify one of these coins by its vernacular name. For instance, every Malayali knows what an "Amâda" is: it is what we know to be a real or imitation Venetian sequin.* The half louis of the empire is known as the "pakshikkas," probably from the eagle on the reverse. And so on.†

Ornaments are never worn on the ankles or on the waist, as is the rule in other parts of Southern India.

Dress, men.—This is very simple; ordinarily one cloth round the loins, the ends overlapping a foot or two in front. It is not tucked between the legs, which is the fashion practically all over India, but hangs straight to the ground. It should touch the ground, or very nearly do so. Wearing a cloth in such fashion carries with it dignity to the wearer. A Tîyan, or a man of any inferior

---

* I have never heard any explanation of the word Amâda in Malabar. The following comes from Tinnevelly: "Amâda was the consort of Bhagavati and he suddenly appeared one day before a Shânár (the caste devoted to climbing the palms and drawing off the juice) and demanded food. The Shânár said he was a poor man with nothing to offer but toddy, which however he gave in a palmyra leaf. Amâda drank the toddy and performing a mantram over the leaf it turned into gold coins which bore on one side the pictures of Amâda, the Shânár and the tree; and these he gave the Shânár on a reward for his willingness to assist him. This explains the two names—Shânár caste (as they are called in Tinnevelly, but where they are not very common), and Amâda."

† It is scarcely right to say any of these coins, even the sequin, is not current. The value of each is known everywhere to a nicety. It must be remembered that throughout Malabar copper coins of the English and Dutch East India Companies, of Mysore, and of almost every former dynasty of South India are to be found amongst the coins actually current with the people, while in the rural parts reckoning is always in fanams: not in annas.

caste, is not supposed to wear his cloth below his knees. Now-a-days, when there is a general levelling up, the inferior races occupying a position they never held before, when people speak of caste as if it were a fanciful arrangement of the social fabric which it would be an excellent thing to destroy, forgetting that, fundamentally, it rests on racial differentiation, we see those of castes inferior to the Nâyar wearing their cloths to the ground—in the towns that is, where the sway of modern officialdom and education is felt. But, were a man of inferior caste to wear his cloth to the ground, away out in the district where the old order has not changed much, he would soon be made to repent having done what is believed to be an infringement of the privileges of the Nâyar. He would probably be well beaten, and might have his house burnt. The single cloth (mundu) constitutes the ordinary dress. No turban is worn. It is wrong for a Nâyar to cover his head. But he may use an umbrella, and invariably does so when walking in the sun, for he is very susceptible to its rays. The cloth must be fastened at the waist in a certain way. Those of every caste tie or fasten their cloth round the loins in a certain way; people of no two castes tie the cloth alike.

Women.—A short cloth is worn somewhat tight round the loins, and over it is worn another cloth from the waist to below the knee. Nothing is worn above waist. When one sees women of the Nâyar caste on the roads (they are *never* to be seen in the towns), or at the festivals or other large gatherings, they are wearing a cloth loosely covering the upper portion of the body. In Malabar, where there is prevalent the idea that no respectable woman covers her breast, there has crept in lately, chiefly amongst those who have travelled, a feeling of shame in respect of this custom of dress. Dress is, of course, a conventional affair, and it will be matter for regret should false ideas of shame supplant those of natural dignity such as one sees expressed in the carriage and bearing of the well-bred Nâyar lady.

It will be most convenient to deal with the Nâyars as a body under such heads as marriage, customs, etc. Here we are concerned mainly with physical measures and general appearance, under which come dress and ornament. What has been said about dress may be taken as descriptive of all the clans. Before leaving the Kiriattil Nâyars it will be well to note the names of some of those actually measured.

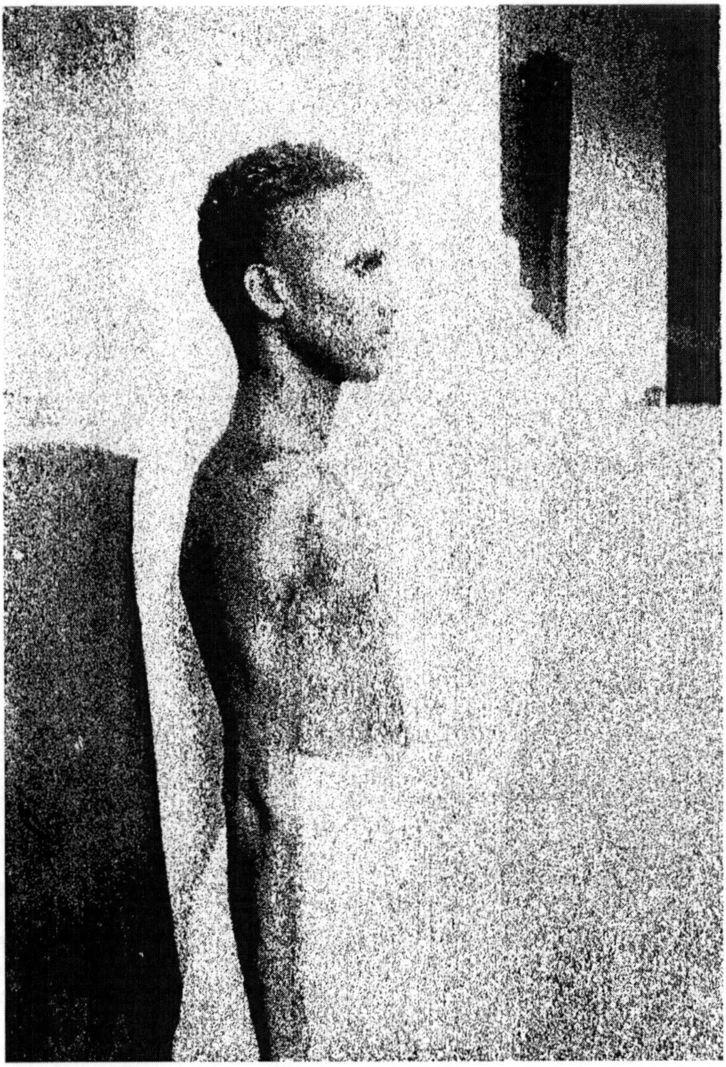

AKATTU CHARNA NAYAR. FATHER A NAMBUTIRI.

Nâyar is affixed as an honorific after the name. Thus one whose name is Gôvindan is called Gôvindan Nâyar.

Taravâd name.	Name.	Occupation.	Age
Manjôli	Gôvindan	Domestic servant ...	30
Kêdôth	Karunâkaran ...	Milk seller	34
Chuliotkolodi	Ithapu	Cultivator	32
Puliakôth	Kêlu	Do.	27
Kurunthal	Narrâinan	Do.	35
Kazhaparambath ...	Shankaren	Do.	32
Etalakandiel	Kêlu	Servant	22
Thanikât	Cherukutti	Do.	25
Thattatath	Chekkunni	Peon	35
Nambidivittil	Kunhunni	Cultivator	50
Nadaviladatha	Chandukutti ..	Do.	25
Tuthenvittil	Vêlu	Writer	24
Thekakamukal	Rámuni	Cultivator	22
Kulangarathathil ...	Kannan	Do.	37
Kizhukalangot	Gôvindan	Do.	25
Pitôli	Rámuni	Do.	36
Puliakôth	Kôman	Do.	25
Edakapura	Rârappan	Peon	46

There seems to be a distinct or specific name for every garden, every acre of land in Malabar, whether in the forest or cultivated, whether enclosed or not. We shall hear of this again when we come to speak of the jungle people, some of whom change their name, their *house* or Taravâd name, as they change their residence from one place to another, always calling themselves after the land on which they are at the time living. Others again cling to the name which is that of the land whence the family has sprung, so to speak.

That the Taravâd name of the Nâyar is that of the land is tolerably evident. Contrary to the rule in Southern India there is, in Malabar, absolute proprietorship of land; and the land, the family house built on it, the land wherein lie the ashes of the ancestors, and the family itself are all included in the meaning of the word Taravâd.

ÚRÂLI NÂYARS: ENDOGAMOUS.

Ages ranging between 20 and 45.	Maximum.	Minimum.	Averages of 25.	To stature = 100.	Remarks
Stature	180·8	152·2	163·1	...	
Height, sitting	89·9	79·1	84·2	51·6	
Do. kneeling ...	135·3	113·3	• 120·8	74·0	• 120·75
Span	193·0	161·7	171·3	105·0	

ÚRÂLI NÂYARS—*cont.*

Ages ranging between 20 and 45.	Maximum.	Minimum.	Averages of 25.	To stature = 100.	Remarks.
Chest	88·0	77·4	81·2	49·8	
Shouldars	43·7	36·8	39·7	24·3	
Left cubit	51·4	41·6	45·2	27·7	
Left hand length ...	20·5	17·0	17·8	10·9	
Do. width	8·8	7·5	7·9	...	
Left middle finger ...	12·2	9·6	10·7	...	
Hips	29·6	23·7	26·0	15·9	
Left foot length	28·3	23·7	24·7	15·1	
Do. width	9·8	8·2	8·7	...	
Cephalic length	20·4	17·5	19·2	11·8	
Do. width	15·0	13·4	14·0	..	
Do. index	79·0	68·2	72·9	...	
Bigoniac	11·1	10·0	10·5	...	
Bizygomatic	13·7	12·2	13·2	...	
Maxillo-zygomatic index.	84·8	74·1	80·6	...	
Nasal height ...	* 5·3	4·1	4·8	2·94	* There were 6 of 5·0 and over.
Do. width	4·0	3·2	3·6	...	
Do. index	84·4	65·4	75·5	..	
Vertex to tragus	14·2	11·9	12·9	7·9	
Do. to chin	21·2	18·4	19·9	12·2	
Middle finger to patella...	18·7	7·1	11·5	7·05	

Face.—Among the descriptive notes of individuals made when measuring them are these:—

(1) Supraciliary arches, slight. Nasal notch. Chin recedes slightly. Chin square with slight hollow in front.

(2) Nasal bone slightly raised. Nasal notch moderate. Supraciliary arches ditto. Chin pointed.

(3) Head pyramidal. Thick flabby nose. Nasal bone slightly raised.

(4) Forehead moderately high and straight. Supraciliary arches slight. Nasal notch. Nose straight; very slight prognathism. Chin recedes.

(5) Forehead high. Supraciliary arches marked. Lips thick. Nasal notch. Nasal bone slightly raised. Ears small.

(6) Protuberance over the right ear. Forehead markedly prominent. No nasal notch.

As a rule the nose is straight, or the nasal bone is slightly raised. In some cases the nasal notch is deep.

In one individual the broadest part of the head was just *above* the ear.

In another, the alæ of the nose appear to have become enlarged through taking snuff.

In another, the point of the ear (noticed by Darwin) in the helix $\frac{1}{3}$ from the top, was very marked.

One individual of 29 looked at least 40. He had suffered severely from small-pox.

Figure.—The average is slight to medium. One is noted as stout, and another as very strongly built.

Hair.—It has been noticed already (see Nambûtiris. Bulletin, Vol. III, No. I) that the growth of hair on the cheeks is a racial characteristic. In some of the lower races it is entirely absent, while in the Nambûtiris it is constant. About half the Urâli Nâyars examined had a regular growth of hair on the cheeks.

On the head.—In all but one the hair on the head, invariably black and glossy, was thick and wavy; in a few, it was very thick or fairly so; and, in the case of three individuals, it was noted as curly. A few grey hairs were noticed in four individuals aged respectively 25, 29, 30, 45; and one young fellow of 20 had a small patch of white hair over the right eyebrow.

Hair on the chest was slight to moderate as a rule, but in 4 individuals it was thick.

Hair on the arms was observed to be slight in 13, and moderate or thick in 12.

In all, the hair on the legs varied between moderate and thick, excepting that in 2 the growth was very thick. One man had shaved his feet, and another had shaved the backs of his hand and his wrists. In a few there was a tolerably thick growth of hair in the small of the back. This is common to all the Nâyars.

Colour of the skin.—In 22 cases in which this was recorded the darkest was No. 43 (Broca's colour types) and the fairest No. 40. Twelve individuals were of No. 29 or fairer, and this (a little fairer than 29) seems to be about the average. A little darker than the Kiriattil.

Colour of the eyes.—8 individuals were of No. 2 (Broca); 6 individuals were of No. 1; 6 individuals between 1 and 2.

Ornaments.—A few of those examined said that men of the clan never wore earrings, though their ears were pierced. There may be some section of the clan who do not; but, as a rule, earrings are worn by those who can afford them. One man indeed said he never wore them, fearing thieves might steal them. Another wore silver earrings called kalluvechcha kadukkan which means an earring set with stone (pushyarâgam—topaz).

(1) Three plain golden rings on ring finger of left hand, the same on the little finger of the same hand, and a thin iron ring on the ring finger of the right hand.

(2) Sandal paste patch over glabella; four stripes of the same on chest; three vertical stripes on each upper arm.

(3) Three golden earrings—the usual kadukkans—in each ear. An amulet in a silver cylindrical case worn on the waist. Inside the case is a charm written on a copper leaf. It is to protect its wearer against the influences of the evil eye.

(4) One tambâk, one plain gold ring on ring finger of the right hand.

(5) Ears pierced. Wears no earrings as he has no money. A dab of sandal paste over the glabella, another over the sternum, and on each shoulder.

Prolificness.—The clan being endogamous, it will be well to note here the number of children born in 16 families of those examined. In all there were born 44 male and 35 female children; altogether 79. This gives an average of 4·9 in each family; and of those there were living at the time an average of 4·6 for each family. A figure which is above the average for the Nâyars as a body, be it noted.

It is perhaps scarcely worth noting that the average weight of four men was 119 lb.

Names of some of those examinad.

Taravâd.	Name.	Occupation.	Age.
Mêlapalli	Kêlu Nâyar	Cooly	22
Kanjôli	Râman Nâyar	Writer	22
Kurundottathil	Krishnan Nâyar	Do.	20
Puthukûdi	Achutan Nâyar	Trade	22
Ponmilli	Krishnan Nâyar	Do.	45
Kuttakil	Râman Nâyar	Cooly	32
Payarvîtil	Aiyappen Nâyar	Mason	36
Pûvakunial	Châthu Nâyar	Cultivator	26
Kalathil	Shangaran Nâyar	Cooly	25
Korolath	Shangunni Nâyar	Do.	22
Pallithotathil	Gôpalan Nâyar	Nothing	22
Kûtakkil	Ràman Nâyar	Cooly	30
Thondil	Appa Nâyar	Writer	20

Thondi or Thundi was, I think, mentioned by one of the ancient geographers as a port near where this last man lived. This man, therefore, bears the name of the place as it was, probably, in the days of Ptolemy.

VATTAKKÂD NÂYARS.

There is some obscurity in the sub-divisions of this clan. To the north of Calicut, in Kurumbranâd, they are divided into the Undiâtuna, or "those who pull" (to work the oil machine by hand) and the "Muri-Vechchu-â tune," or "those who tie or fasten bullocks" (to work the oil machine by means of bullocks and not by hand); yet farther north, Tellicherry and thereabouts there are no known sub-divisions; while in Ernâd, to the eastward, these names are quite unknown, and the clan is divided into the "Veluttâtu," the White, and the "Karuttâtu," the Black. It has been remarked already (page 82) that the Vattakkâd (those who turn round) are not always admitted to be true Nâyars. In the extreme north of Malabar they are called Vaniyan—oil monger. The "White" have nothing to do with expression and preparation of oil, which is the hereditary occupation of the Black. The "White" may eat with Nâyars of any clan; the Black can eat with no others outside their own clan. The Black sub-clan is strictly endogamous. The other, the superior sub-clan, is not. Their woman may marry with men of any other clan, the Pallichchan excepted. But not *vice versâ*. The men must marry within their own sub-clan. I think, but am not sure a man of this clan may marry a woman of the Pallichchan clan; but even if such an alliance is permissible anywhere, I do not think it ever takes place. It may be taken as accurate that men of the clan always marry within their own sub-clan, and that women of the superior sub-clan very often mate with Nâyars of superior clans.

In taking the measures I made no distinction between the sub-clans; it was only just before completion that the existence of the sub-clans was discovered. Had the important fact been discovered earlier, the sub-clans would have been separated. Though scarcely enough for scientific accuracy, it is tolerably certain that most, if not all, of those examined were of the superior sub-clan, which is exogamous as regards the women. The inferior section of the clan—the Black—is not to be found north of the Korapuzha river in North Malabar. One quarter of my subjects were measured in North Malabar—Cannanore, Tellicherry, Badagara; and for the rest, in some cases it is noted that the individuals are of the superior section. This accounts pretty correctly for rather more than half. I am tolerably certain that the other half also belonged to it.

However alert one's discrimination may be, one may fall into possible error as I did here. "What caste do you belong to?" "I am a Nâyar." "What kind of Nâyar?" "I am a Nâyar." It may take some time to let in comprehension that the name of his clan is wanted, then the answer is "I am a good Nâyar" (one of a good or superior clan). At last he will say he is a Sûdra Nâyar, a Kiriyattil or whatever he may be. Again, many claim the Kiriyattil as their clan when they really have no right to do so, being inferior to it.

Ages ranging between 20 and 62.	Maximum.	Minimum.	Averages of 25.	To stature = 100.
Stature	178·6	154·3	167·0	...
Height, sitting	92·0	78·7	84·6	50·6
Do. kneeling	131·3	112·4	122·9	73·6
Span	190·0	164·7	177·8	106·5
Chest	95·8	70·6	81·3	48·7
Shoulders	42·8	36·9	40·3	24·1
Left cubit	51·4	44·3	46·9	28·1
Left hand, length	20·5	17·0	18·7	11·2
Do. width	8·9	7·6	8·2	...
Do. middle finger	12·6	10·4	11·9	...
Hips	27·8	23·6	26·3	15·7
Left foot length	28·1	23·6	25·7	15·4
Do. width	9·8	7·9	8·9	...
Cephalic length	20·1	18·2	19·2	11·5
Do. width	15·0	13·2	14·2	...
Do. index	79·0	68·0	74·0	...
Bigoniac	11·2	9·7	10·5	...
Bizygomatic	14·0	12·3	13·1	...
Maxillo-zygomatic index ...	84·4	77·0	80·1	...
Nasal height	5·3	4·0	4·9	2·93
Do. width	3·9	3·0	3·5	...
Do. index	87·5	61·2	73·1	...
Vertex to tragus	13·9	12·3	13·1	7·8
Do. to chin	21·5	17·3	19·8	11·9
Middle finger to patella	14·5	1·8	9·4	5·62

The individual, whose mid finger when standing at "attention" to the top of his patella gives the maximum measure, had a span which was 23·4 more than his height. In seven, the length of the left foot was greater than the breadth of the hips across the crests of the ilium. In ten, the nasal length was 5 cm. and over.

The statures of the first ten measured averaged 168·2 and the nasal index 76·6; otherwise the correspondence between the averages of 10 and of 25 is complete. Perhaps mixture of subjects belonging to the two sections of the clan is responsible for the rather important differences noted.

Face.—Nasal notch is noted as deep in 3 and moderate in 1; in the others it was slight or not apparent. The nasal bone was raised above the line of the nose in 5, and depressed in 2. The following are brief notes of individuals:—

(1) Deep nasal notch. Forehead high. Supraciliary arches very slight. Chin long.

(2) Forehead high. Nasal point slightly raised. Nasal notch moderate.

(3) Nasal point depressed so that the nose has as it were a knob at the tip.

(4) Supraciliary arches not apparent to the touch. Slightly rounded nostrils. Teeth project forwards.

(5) Deep nasal notch. Supraciliary arches marked.

The posterior portion of the head of the individual whose nasal index was the minimum seemed to project uncommonly; but his cephalic length was no more than 19·4 or a little above the average.

Figure.—Two-thirds are noted as "slight," nearly one-third as "medium," and two (individuals) as stout. One was very lean.

Hair.—In rather more than half the number of subjects the hair on the head was noted as *thick* and *wavy*. In most of the others it was *moderately thick*. In two only it was thin. In two it was *curly*. A man aged 27 had very slight growth of hair on the face (none on the cheeks), but had a fairly strong growth in the small of the back. Individuals of 40, 42 and 62 were a little grey, while one of 45 was almost bald, and what hair he had was white. Very few had hair on the cheeks, or anything like a full growth thereof. It was observed in but two instances, and in a third as slight. But it is proper to remark that, in the earlier period of my investigations, I did not make special notes about whiskers.

Hair on the chest is, as usual, not easy to gauge when there obtains the custom of shaving it periodically, every fortnight or every month. In about a quarter of the subjects the growth is noted as moderate, and in a sixth as thick; in the rest as slight or very slight. In the case of a man aged 45 the hair was white as well as thick.

Hair on the arms was moderate to thick in 13, slight to very slight in 11, and absent in 1.

Hair on the legs was, in every case but one, moderate or thick; in the case of one, very thick. The exception was in the case of a man sick and ill developed.

Colour of the skin (Broca's colour types).—The fairest was No. 40 (one only); and the two next fairest were 30 to 44 and 39 to 44. The darkest was 43. The average seems to be a little darker than 29 but not so dark as 28. Darker than the Kiriyattil.

Colour of the eyes (Broca).—The colour of the eyes of half the number was as No. 1, and that of the other half as No. 2. One exception was between Nos. 1 and 10. The average therefore is a dark brown; not black.

Ornaments.—Ears pierced, and the usual earrings (kadukkans) worn by those who can afford them. In one case the earrings were set with a red stone. The ornaments or adornments of various individuals were as follows:—

(1) Bell metal ring on the ring finger of right hand.

(2) Two brass rings on ring finger of right hand. A string of wool thrice round the right wrist to keep off fever at night.

(3) Tattooed circular mark over glabella. The operator was a woman of the Chetti caste, a travelling tattooer, and the cost of the operation 2 pies.

(4) One gold kadukkan in each ear. Two copper rings on ring finger of right hand. Washing the face with a hand wearing a copper ring removes black spots on the face, and prevents them coming. So said the wearer.

(5) Two amulets, silver cylindrical cases containing mantrams, worn on a string round the waist to keep off fever and devils. Amulet cases are often worn on the waist in the way of ornament pure and simple.

Prolificness.—In 12 families the children born were 29 males and 34 females, or an average of 5·2 children to each family.

The average weight of 4 individuals was 119½ lb.

The names of some of those examined.

Taravâd.	Name.	Occupation.	Age.
Blathâdi ...	Govindan ...	Cultivator ...	40
Râvâri Chandil ...	Kêlu ...	Do. ...	22
Palôli ...	Kunju ...	Do. ...	25
Murikolipôil ...	Shangaran ...	Trader ...	21
Kuttadath ...	Krishnan ...	Writer ...	20
Thaikandi ...	Appu ...	Cooly ...	26
Thazhathadathil ...	Châthu ...	Do. ...	24
Erankulangara ...	Kittan ...	Milk seller ...	25
Vêlashêri ...	Cherukoman ...	Cultivator ...	40
Chêlattumal ...	Kunhunni ...	Cooly ...	44
Patavetti ...	Châthukutti ...	Cultivator ...	62

SÛDRA NÂYARS.

We now come to the Sûdra Nâyars, men and women of which clan supply the house servants in the Nambûtiri Brâhmans' houses. It is only a few who are occupied in this way, however, and of all those examined only one is noted as a servant. The subjects were found in various parts of South Malabar, a few from the neighbouring Cochin Native State.

Ages ranging between 22 and 52.	Maximum.	Minimum.	Averages of 25.	To stature =100.
Stature	173·3	151·1	165·9	...
Height, sitting	90·8	78·8	85·8	51·7
Do. kneeling	128·3	110·1	122·9	74·1
Span	186·0	158·3	174·3	105·1
Chest	89·0	76·0	81·1	48·7
Shoulders	43·4	37·4	40·2	24·2
Left cubit	48·6	41·4	46·1	27·3
Left hand, length	20·8	16·8	18·7	11·3
Do. width	8·6	7·3	8·1	...
Left middle finger	12·1	9·9	11·1	..
Hips	27·9	24·0	26·0	15·7
Left foot, length	27·0	23·1	25·3	15·3
Do. width	10·3	7·8	8·9	...
Cephalic length	20·2	17·7	19·2	11·6
Do. width	15·3	13·0	14·1	...
Do. index	86·4	65·0	73·8	...
Bigoniac	11·4	9·4	10·5	...
Bizygomatic	14·1	11·9	13·1	...
Maxillo-zygomatic index	85·7	76·6	80·3	.
Nasal height	5·4	4·0	4·7	2·83
Do. width	4·2	3·3	3·7	...
Do. index	89·1	67·9	79·4	...
Vertex to tragus	14·4	12·5	13·3	8·0
Do. to chin	21·3	17·7	19·6	11·8
Middle finger to patella	15·7	7·0	9·9	5·97

Note.—The individual whose cephalic index is the maximum was measured in Palghat, where there are many Pattar (East Coast) Brâhmans; his father was, in all probability, one of them. The index of no other equalled 79·0. One broad headed man, whose father was known to have been a Pattar Brâhman, was excluded from the averages.

There were but three subjects whose nasal height was 5 cm. and over.

Face.—Slight prognathism was noticed in one. In another the posterior portion of the parietal was curiously flat.

Some individuals were described in my notes—

(1) Nasal bones wide and thick. Teeth project.

(2) Lips thick and somewhat projecting. Chin receding. The flesh on the chin is thick, giving it a rounded lump like appearance. Inion appears to be in a projecting ridge round the back of the head. (Cephalic length 19·7.)

(3) Supraciliary arches slight. Nasal notch. Nose straight. Lips slightly everted. Teeth in upper jaw project forwards. Eyes deep set. Inner corner of eyes a trifle oblique.

The last two specimens are uncommon; not typical. The thick lips and projecting teeth are not usually noticeable as in their case. The long oval face is the common type. The fashion of wearing no hair on the face, shaving the head at the back and at the sides and a little over the forehead, leaving but the oval patch on the vertex, no head covering being worn, gives the face an appearance of length. But while the average of the measure vertex to chin, for all the Nâyars,* reduced to stature equals 100, is 11·9, the same for 21 of the 30 different castes † examined in Malabar is greater. The Mukkuvan is as high as 13·4, while on the other hand the Nambûtiri is less, being but 11·7.

Figure.—One out of 25 is recorded as "stout." One-third were "slight." Nearly two-thirds were medium or thereabouts; and this seems to represent the average.

Hair.—More than half are noted as having whiskers, that is, growth of hair on the cheeks. In two-thirds of the subjects the hair on the head was thick and wavy; in a few cases it was very thick. Individuals aged respectively 25, 32, and 52 were noted as being a little grey. In one-quarter of the total number the hair was thin to moderately thick. One individual of this clan is marked as having hair a little grey.

Hair on the chest.—Rather more than a quarter of the whole had thick to moderately thick hair. In the case of one man hair was thick all over the body, even on the back: everywhere except over the ribs, the front of the upper arm and shoulder. In another the hair on the small of the back was *thick*. In the greater number of individuals it was marked slight, and moderate, and in a few it was absent.

* Group A included.

† Counting each clan of the Nâyars separately.

Hair on the arms.—In half the number of subjects it varied from moderate to thick; in the other half it was slight to very slight or (in a few) absent altogether.

Hair on the legs.—In more than half it varied from moderately thick to very thick. One was noted as "like a bear." In one individual only it was noted as very slight.

Colour of the skin.—The darkest (one only) was between 42 and 43 (Broca's colour types). Two others were nearly as dark. The fairest was 44. Two others were nearly as fair. The average is between these extremes.

Colour of the eyes.—The darkest was No. 1 (Broca's colour types). The lightest between 2 and 3. Rather more than half were 2 or shades of 2, generally lighter, while nearly one-half were No. 1.

Ornaments.—As a rule the ordinary earrings are worn. A section of the clan calling themselves Ellenkiria (or Elleng Kiria—tender Kiria?) wear no earrings, though their ears are pierced. Some members of this section told me they never wore earrings, while others said they could wear them as a rule, but they could not wear them when they went to the Kôvilakam (palace) of the Zamorin.

The right nostril of one man was slit vertically as if for insertion of a jewel. His mother miscarried in her first pregnancy, so, according to custom, he, the child of her second pregnancy, had had his nose slit.

Another wore a silver bangle. He had had a wound on his arm which was long in healing, so made a vow to the God at Tirupati (North Arcot District) that, if his arm was healed, he would give up the bangle at the Tirupati temple. He intended to *send* the bangle by a messenger, any one going to Tirupati, when his arm was quite healed: then only would he fulfil his vow. If this illustrates how a vow *may* be fulfilled,—he had not vowed to go *himself* and give the bangle up, only to *give* the bangle which was meanwhile convenient as an ornament,—the man's ideas about the God at Tirupati illustrate the confused ideas as to the personality and attributes of the Gods of Modern Hinduism which obtain in Malabar. He thought it was Baghavati whose shrine was the object of pilgrimage to Tirupati, but was not at all sure; indeed he was not sure whether it was a God or a Goddess. It is scarcely necessary to say that the God at Tirupati is a form of Vishnu.

Other individuals wore ornaments, thus—

(1) Gold ring on ring-finger of the left hand. Earrings with red stone. Amulet against the evil eye.

Copper sheet on which the charm was inscribed in a silver cylindrical case. Copper ring on ring-finger, right hand.

(2) Two copper rings on the ring-finger, right hand. Belongs to the Ellenkiria, so wore no earrings.

(3) Brass ring, ring-finger, right hand. Also of the Ellenkiria.

(4) Copper ring, ring-finger, right hand. Gold earrings of the ordinary pattern.

(5) The ordinary gold earrings. Silver string round the waist; not exclusively ornamental. He fastened his loin cloth to it.

Vital Statistics were noted in but two cases. In one family there were two brothers and three sisters; in another, one brother and two sisters.

Names, etc., of a few Taravâd.	Name.	Occupation.	Age.
Puthen Vîtil	Krishnan	Cultivator	52
Paritbil	Achutan	Do.	27
Malabîtil	Sivarâman	Do.	22
Cholale	Râman	Do.	20
Muthîra	Narrâyanan	Teacher	26
Kanakath	Kunhi Krishnan * ...	Unemployed ...	22
Mannareth	Shangaran	Trader	30
Kûmbiyal	Kannan	Peon	25
Othianmâdattil ...	Gôvindan	Do.	33

NAMBIYÂR NÂYARS.

Men of this clan affix Nambiyâr to their name. Thus, Gôvindan Nambiyâr, Kêlu Nambiyâr.

Ages ranging between 20 and 40.	Maximum.	Minimum.	Averages of 22.	To stature = 100.
Stature	177·1	155·7	165·1	...
Height, sitting	89·3	80·0	84·2	51·0
Do. kneeling	129·8	115·0	122·0	73·9
Span	188·0	166·5	175·3	106·2
Chest	84·0	75·0	80·3	48·6
Shoulders	42·8	37·8	40·0	424·2
Left cubit	50·5	43·6	46·0	27·9

* This individual had 'Menon' instead of Nâyar after his name, he having been invested with the distinction by the Zamorin.

NAYAR WOMEN (SOUTH MALABAR), AGED 20 AND 17.

NAMBIYÂR NÂYARS—*cont.*

Ages ranging between 20 and 40.	Maxi-mum.	Mini-mum.	Aver-ages of 22.	To stature = 100.
Left hand length	20·0	17·7	18·4	...
Do. width	8·5	7·3	7·8	...
Do. middle finger ...	12·5	10·3	10·9	...
Hips	26·7	24·4	25·4	15·4
Left foot length	27·2	23·6	25·2	15·3
Do. width	9·2	8·0	8·6	...
Cephalic length	20·6	18·3	19·2	11·6
Do. width	15·4	13·2	14·1	...
Do. index	79·3	69·4	73·7	...
Bigoniac	11·5	9·1	10·3	...
Bizygomatic	13·5	11·9	13·0	...
Maxillo-zygomatic index ...	87·1	73·8	79·2	...
Nasal height	5·5	4·2	4·8	...
Do. width	4·3	3·2	3·7	...
Do. index	92·9	62·7	77·3	...
Vertex to tragus	13·9	12·2	13·0	7·9
Do. to chin	21·4	18·2	19·7	11·9
Mid finger to patella	15·7	6·5	10·4	4·73

Note.—Although the number of subjects is limited to 22, the averages may be accepted as correct. The averages for 10 and for 25 are, as a rule, identical; in a few there is a trifling difference, but nowhere is the difference more than trifling.

In eight individuals the nasal height was 5 cm. or over. This is about 36 per cent.

In four the nasal index was 90 or over, and in four it was less than 70.

Face.—Observation was recorded in but nine instances.

The reason for this which seems to give examination of subjects a somewhat casual character, is that during the early part of my investigations my notes as to physical characteristics, shape of the nose, etc., were less complete than they were later on. Very seldom, in fact only in the case of the Irulans, was one caste examined completely at a time. It was impossible to work on the people caste by caste. Official duties rendered it impossible to regulate one's peregrinations so as to do so. Subjects were taken where and when they could be got hold of anywhere in the district.

In two cases only the supraciliary arches were rather prominent; in the others, slight or absent.

In four the nasal point was somewhat elevated. Slight prognathism with projecting teeth was observed in one individual, an unhealthy person.

Figure.—Seventy-one per cent. of the subjects were noted as "slight," 29 per cent. as "medium" and of those but two individuals are put down as "sturdily built."

Hair.—In three individuals hairiness was conspicuously apparent, there being hair nearly all over the body, and in one of these the hair in the small of the back was so thick that in my notes it is described as "like a bush."

On the head.—In nearly 80 per cent. of the subjects the hair on the head was "plentiful and wavy"; in a few of these it was "very thick," while in the remaining 20 per cent. it was "moderate." In no case was it noted as "thin" or "slight." The number of subjects in which growth of hair on the cheeks was noted was one-fifth of the whole.

On the chest.—In nearly a quarter, the hair on the chest was noted as "thick."

On the arms.—In most cases it varied from "very slight" to "moderate." Rarely "thick."

On the legs.—In nearly half it was "moderately thick" to "thick"; in the remainder, slight to moderate.

Colour of the skin.—It should have been noticed before that the colour of the face of the ordinary Malayali is invariably lighter than that of the body; possibly from the prevailing custom of using the umbrella. Malabar is for the most part shaded by trees and palms, and its peoples have not that disregard for the sun's javelins which we see in the country to the eastward. No one starts on a journey, and rarely leaves his house, without his umbrella—the thing of cadjan now being by degrees replaced by the cheap umbrella of European manufacture. The labourer working in the field, the fisherman in his boat on the sea, the boat-man on the backwater, all wear a large umbrella-like hat. Women always carry an umbrella out of doors; or, as in North Malabar, an umbrella hat-like thing which seems to be a curious survival of the custom of wearing an umbrella hat, is carried. This is, apparently, an ordinary umbrella hat, but the central part, which appears to be made to fit the head, as in the ordinary umbrella hat, is too small by half to fit any head, and this hat-like umbrella is carried in the hand to shield the head from the sun and the face from the inquisitive passer-by. The fact remains that the Nâyar, of whom we are now speaking, who never or very rarely wears any covering on the head, cannot withstand the effect of the direct rays of the sun without an umbrella. A few hours' walk in the midday sun where there is little or no shade, is sufficient to bring on fever to the ordinarily strong man.

Colour of the skin was taken generally on the right arm just below the shoulder, the book containing the colour types being pressed against the skin.

The fairest was No. 44 (Broca).

The darkest was No. 28 (only one of this).

More than half were 29 and fairer, and the remainder were still fairer, several being 44 or very nearly.

Colour of the eyes.—In about three quarters of the subjects the colour of the eyes was No. 2 (Broca); in about one-quarter they were 1 to a trifle darker. In one individual the colour was between 2 and 3; a light brown.

Ornaments.—One or two golden kadukkans are commonly worn in each ear by those who can afford them. Ears pierced always. Though not for purposes of ornament, the ears of two individuals were marked by holes—pieces cut out of the cartilage. In one there was a circular hole 4 mm. in diameter, cut out of the cartilage of the right ear, and in another a circular hole 6 mm. in diameter in the left ear. In both cases the holes had been made during childhood to prevent colic.

The ornaments worn by a few individuals were as follows:—

(1) One tambâk ring on ring finger, right hand. One iron ring on the little finger of the left hand.

(2) One gold kadukkan in each ear. One plain gold ring on the ring finger of the right hand. Wore a silver girdle on the waist instead of a string, to which he fastened his lunguti.

(3) Silver cord round the waist; on it a silver amulet case, of the usual shape, having inside it a charm written on a gold leaf to protect the wearer against the evil eye.

(4) One silver ring on ring finger of the left hand. Two gold kadukkans in each ear.

Miscellaneous.—One man was tested, and found to have perfect vision. Weight was recorded in five cases only; the average was nearly 110 lb. which is probably not far from the general average.

Names, etc., of some of those who were examined are given below:—

Taravâd.	Name.	Occupation.	Age.
Pathushêri ...	... Kanâran ...	... Rent Collector (for a temple).	22
Mâvila ...	... Kumâran ...	... Cultivator	21
Châlayil Kandôth ...	Châttu ...	... .	22
Puthiotil ...	... Râman ...	... Servant	22
Chalil Kannôth	... Anandan ...	... Cultivator	25
Ramath ...	... Kunhi Râman	... Landlord ...	34
Kalliat-panôli	... Râmuni ...	... Stamp vendor ...	30
Thêrugandi ...	... Paidal ...	... Cultivator	25

PURATTU CHÂRNA NÂYARS.

Men of this clan bear the affix Nâyar after their name, as Gôvindan Nâyar, Gôpâla Nâyar.

Ages ranging between 20 and 70.	Maximum.	Minimum.	Averages of 25.	To stature = 100.
Stature	174·8	155·0	166·1	...
Height, sitting	92·4	77·7	85·3	51·3
Do. kneeling	130·2	113·7	122·7	73·9
Span	184·1	155·6	174·0	104·7
Chest	87·6	69·7	79·6	47·9
Shoulders	43·9	33·3	39·6	23·9
Left cubit	49·1	42·0	45·8	27·6
Left hand length	19·3	16·8	18·5	11·1
Do. width	8·3	6·5	7·9	...
Do. middle finger	11·6	9·8	10·5	6·3
Hips	28·0	23·8	25·7	15·5
Left foot length	27·4	22·3	25·3	15·2
Do. width	9·9	7·4	8·7	...
Cephalic length	20·6	17·6	19·5	11·7
Do. width	15·5	12·9	14·5	...
Do. index	81·5	65·2	72·2	...
Bigoniac	11·1	9·3	10·3	...
Bizygomatic	13·9	11·7	13·0	...
Maxillo-zygomatic index	88·8	73·9	79·5	...
Nasal height	5·2	4·0	4·8	2·88
Do. width	3·9	2·9	3·6	2·17
Do. index	90·0	56·9	76·8	...
Vertex to tragus	14·4	12·2	13·1	7·9
Do. to chin	21·1	17·5	19·8	11·9
Middle finger to patella	17·5	5·3	10·7	6·44

Cephalic length.—In 8 individuals or 32 per cent. of the whole, the cephalic length was 20·0 or over. The maximum cephalic width (of one individual only) is abnormal; the next nearest to it is 14·8. In 6 individuals the nasal length was 5 cm. or over. In one individual the iliac bone was much higher at the right side than on the left.

Face.—A few individuals were noted thus—

(1) Deep nasal notch. Nasal point slightly elevated. Helix of ear very thin; the Darwin's point in the centre of the curve on the left and high up on the right.

(2) Deep nasal notch. Chin receding. Lips thick.

(3) Slight nasal notch. Supraciliary arches developed at outer edges. Chin recedes.

(4) Supraciliary arches and glabella in one marked ridge. Nasal point somewhat raised. Nasal notch.

(5) Very deep nasal notch. Very wide and thick eyebrows.

Figure.—More than half are marked as slight—a few of them "very slight"; the rest "medium." None "stout."

Hair.—As a rule, to which exceptions are very few, hair on the head is thick and wavy: curly in the case of one individual. The hair of a man of 70 was noted as "very thin and grey." A man of 31 also had hair which was "thin and grey," but he was exceptional. The growth of hair on the cheeks—whiskers—was observed in almost every subject.

Hair on the chest.—The average is "moderate."

On the arms.—The growth of hair in half of the subjects was "slight to very slight"; in the other half, "moderate to thick."

On the legs.—It was noted as "moderate" to "thick" in more than three-fourths of those examined; in a few, "slight."

The growth of hair of a few individuals is here specified—

(1) Aged 54. Hair on the head moderately thick and grey. Hair on the face white. Growth of hair on the cheeks. Hair all over chest grey. Very long thick hair on the back. Hair on the legs and arms thick.

(2) Aged 36. Hair on the head moderately thick and wavy. Glossy black. On chest and middle line of abdomen, moderate. On the arms and legs moderately thick. Shaves the head (except the crown), face, chest, abdomen, wrists and hands, about every 15 days.

(3) Aged 28. Hair on the head thick and wavy. Growth of hair on cheeks; on the chin it is very thick. On the chest, moderate; on the arms, very slight; on the legs, thick. Does not shave his chest, as doing so would make him weak; on the other hand, if he does not shave his head and face, he will become sick.

Shaving cannot be done on a Tuesday or a Saturday, or on the day of an eclipse of sun or moon; nor on the full moon day, the new moon day, nor on the 11th day of the moon—the Êkadasi. This applies to most Nâyars, but not to all.

Colour of the skin.—The skin of the darkest individual corresponded to Broca's colour type No. 43. There was but one of this colour.

Three were of No. 28.

Seventeen were of No. 29 and lighter.

Three were of No. 37 and lighter.

One not taken.

The average colour must be nearly as fair as 37.

Colour of the eyes.—The average corresponds rather to Broca's No. 2 than to his No. 1.

Nine individuals were of No. 1.

Seven individuals were between 1 and 2.

Seven individuals were of No. 2.

Two not taken.

Ornaments.—All those examined had had their ears pierced; but most of them wore no earrings, saying it was not proper for a Purattu Chârna Nâyar to wear them. Four individuals, or nearly one-sixth of the whole, however, wore the ordinary earrings; one indeed wore (the only instance) one gold and one silver earring in each ear. Rings of any kind may be worn on the fingers, and the thin iron ring such as is usually worn, was observed occasionally on the ring finger of the right hand, or on the little finger of the left.

The ornaments worn by a few individuals were as follows:—

(1) Aged 23. Two rings on the ring finger of the right hand; one of them tambâk (described already), the other of silver and iron. The last was worn as a prophylactic against fever. Said he had worn it for the previous five days, and during that period he had had no fever! (This individual, by the way, had been vaccinated, and suffered from an attack of small-pox nine years afterwards.)

(2) Aged 35. One copper ring on the ring finger of the right hand. An amulet of tiger's teeth (as in my collection) on a string round the waist. The amulet contains nothing, and is worn to protect its wearer from fever. Two silver amulet cases of the usual cylindrical pattern worn on the waist; each contains a mantram written on paper for protection against evil spirits. On

one occasion he was frightened when near water, and subsequently was troubled by beings called Pûtams, devils of a very inferior kind which haunt water. He had bad dreams, so consulted a Mâppila priest (a Musaliar —a priest of sorts) who gave him the mantrams. Wore also a charm—"to entice the public" as he explained, so that people will, as a rule, like him, please him, flatter rather than annoy him. He got this too from a Mâppila priest—a Mullah.

(3) Aged 24. This man had travelled. At Dvâraka the city of Krishna, the ninth incarnation of Vishnu (in the Kulluva peninsula), a chank above and a chakkra below had been branded on his left upper arm, on his right, a chank above and a lotus below. Each forearm bore the branded mark of an indistinct seal said to represent Krishna, testifying to a visit to the temple at Dharnidara. Had been to Benares and worshipped his ancestors at Gaya (throwing their ashes into the Ganges), an operation which at once removes all necessity to give them any further attention.

Prolificness.—In 9 families, in respect of which notes were taken, there were born altogether 48 children, 30 male and 18 female, or about 53 children to each family.

Following the rule, or rather custom, which governs all marital connexions amongst the Nâyars, a woman of this clan may be mated with a man of the same clan, or with a man of the Kiriyattil clan, but with no other clan. Consequently, a man of this clan cannot be mated with a Kiriyattil woman, for the woman can never mate with one who is not at least her equal.

Names of some of those examined.

Taravâd.	Name.	Occupation.	Age.
Kizhâk Vellat	Kundu	Cultivator	42
Panôli	Konti	Do.	22
Karuthôdiyil	Gôvindan Kutti	Head of his family	21
Vellât	Gôpâlan	Cultivator	24
Pudieth	Kanaran	Schoolmaster	23
Puttikapureth	Kelukkutti Menon*	Writer	36
Karumuthil	Kandar, *alias* Kunja Panikkar.*	Cultivator	70
Pâlat	Râma Panikkar	Do.	56
Kâkkât	Gôvindan	Do.	20

* The affix (Panikkar, Menon) is a title, not necessarily but possibly hereditary.

Note.—I find I have noted one man as Viyyâr Purattu Chârna, as if Viyyûr is a sub-clan, and that he marries in his own sub-clan; but I am not sure whether the Puratttu Chârnas are so sub-divided, and think not.

AKATTU CHÂRNA NÂYARS.

This is one of the relatively inferior clans. It is not one of the fighting clans, as the Purattu Chârna. The clan is divided into two sub-clans, one of which looks to the Zamorin as their lord, and the other owns lordship to minor lordlings, as the Tirumulpâd of Nilambûr. The former are superior; and a woman of the latter may mate with a man of the former, but not *vice versâ*. The men, but not the women of the two sub-clans, may eat together. There is no distinctive name for the sub-clans. As mentioned already, women of this clan are under no restriction as to residence or travel as are those of the superior clans; hence, of late, officials in North Malabar, officials or vakils residing in Madras, have been wiving with these women. The women may mate with men of their own or of any other clan or with a Nambûtiri. Not so the men, who can marry women of their own clan only.

Ages ranging from 20 to 44.	Maximum.	Minimum.	Averages of 25.	To stature = 100.	Remarks.
Stature ...	179·4	154·7	165·0	...	
Height, sitting ..	92·0	79·7	85·5	51·8	
Do. kneeling ...	132·6	113·8	122·3	72·1	
Span ...	190·4	161·9	175·2	106·2	
Chest ...	89·0	76·6	81·0	49·0	
Shoulders ...	42·5	37·4	40·1	24·3	
Left cubit ...	51·1	42·4	45·9	27·8	
Left hand length ...	21·2	16·9	18·4	*11·1	* 11·15
Do. width ...	8·8	7·3	8·0	..	
Left middle finger ...	12·7	10·1	10·9	6·6	
Do. hips Do. ...	28·4	24·1	25·9	15.7	
Left foot length ...	28·7	22·3	†25·1	15·2	† 25·15. In one subject greatest length was measured to the second toe.
Do. width ...	9·8	7·9	8·8	...	
Cephalic length ...	20·4	17·0	19·1	11·6	
Do. width ...	15·5	13·0	13·9	...	
Do. index ...	80·6	67·2	72·8	...	
Bigoniac ...	11·2	9·8	10·5	...	
Bizygomatic ...	14·2	11·8	13·0	...	
Maxillo-zygomatic index.	85·4	78·5	81·2	...	
Nasal height ...	5·4	4·0	4·7	2·84	
Do. width ...	4·1	3·1	3·6	...	
Do. index ...	90·9	63·0	77·0		
Vertex to tragus ...	13·9	11·8	12·9	7·9	
Do. to chin ...	20·9	17·9	19·6	11·9	
Middle finger to patella.	13·5	3·3	9·9	5·97	

In three the cephalic length was 20 cm. or over. In nine the nasal height was 5 cm. or over.

Face.—The notes made on a few individuals will be set down here. In most cases the supraciliary arches were well marked, and the nasal notch was deep. Nose generally straight, or nasal point slightly raised. Prognathism rare. Lips, especially the lower lip, often very thick.

(1) Very well bred looking. Eyebrows fleshy and thickly marked. Supraciliary arches very slight. Deep nasal notch. Nose straight; nasal point raised very slightly—and very well shaped. In the left ear a very small hole above the usual one in the lobe; I have not noted why it was made.

(2) Supraciliary arches rather prominent. Upper portion of forehead somewhat protuberant. Deep nasal notch. Nasal point raised. Lower lip thick. This man's father was a Nambûtiri. He appears in the plate.

(3) Forehead high. Deep nasal notch. Slight prognathism. Lower lip very thick.

(4) Supraciliary arches not marked. Nasal notch moderate. Lips thin.

Two out of the twenty-five were deeply pitted with small-pox, the Malabar goddess of small-pox, Bhânnâramûrti, having hurt them. In one man the broadest part of the head was above the ears, a little in front.

Figure.—The number of those put down as slight and those put down as medium are about equal.

Hair.—Worn in the usual Malayali fashion which has been described already and, as a rule, plentiful and wavy; treated with gingelly oil, which is sometimes perfumed. The number of individuals whose hair (on the head) was noted as "very thick and wavy" is abnormally large. A young man aged 24 had some white hairs here and there on his head; a man of 35 was a little grey; a man of 39 also; and one of 44 was quite grey. Whiskers or growth of hair on the cheeks were observed in more than half the number of subjects. In several there was hair, fairly thick in some, in the small of the back, and one man had thick hair all over the back.

Hair on the chest was "moderate" or "thick" in more than half.

Hair on the arms was "moderate to thick" in about half; in the other half "slight."

Hair on the legs was, as a rule, thick: rarely less than moderately thick. The legs of one man were like those of a bear.

The hair on the person of a youth aged 20 (No. 1 above) was noted thus—

(*a*) On the head very plentiful, black, glossy and wavy; treated with gingelly oil. Sprouting on the lip and chin. A small patch of moderate thickness on the sternum; slight on the arms; moderate on the legs.

Another, aged 25—

(*b*) On the head very thick, and approaching the outer edge of the eyebrows. Thick on the chest and mid line of abdomen, although these parts have been shaved recently, as also the arm pits. Thick hair in the small of the back. Slight growth on the back. Moderate on the arms; thick on the legs.

The individual (*a*) said he shaved any day of the week, and any day of the month. He was the Kârnavan of his Taravâd: a very youthful one.

Colour of the skin.—The fairest was between 33 and 40 (Broca); the darkest was 43 (redder). The average seems to be between 29, 37 and 44.

Colour of the eyes is a light brown. The actual numbers are—

Of colour type	No.	1	(Broca)	5	individuals.
,,	,,	,,	1 to 2	,,	6	,,
,,	,,	,,	2	,,	7	,,
,,	,,	,,	2 to 3	,,	5	,,

(Two were not included.) So that, although the eyes of rather more than one-fifth were dark brown, what would ordinarily be called black, the remainder were distinctly lighter in colour; and the number of persons whose eyes might be called quite a light brown, equalled those whose eyes were nearly black.

Weight of but 3 was recorded. The average is 105½ lb.

Prolificness.—In the 8 recorded instances the average number of children in each family was 3·7. It will be remembered that this clan is perhaps most of all under process of intermixture, its women mating with men of several higher clans (their own included) and with Nambûtiris.

Ornaments.—Ears are always pierced, and the usual Malabar earrings—kadukkans—are worn; sometimes as many as four in each ear. Individuals were noted thus—

(1) Aged 24. Circular patch of sandalwood paste, 1·8 cms. in diameter over the glabella. Two stripes of sandalwood paste on each upper arm. No ornaments.

PL. X.

JEWELLERY WORN BY NAYAR WOMEN.

(2) Aged 32. Four gold earrings in each ear. One "tambâk" ring on ring finger of left hand. A ring made of a bit of wire picked up on the road worn on the ring finger of left hand.

(3) Two gold earrings, set with a red stone, in each ear. Wears an amulet, contained in the ordinary cylindrical amulet case; but I have not noticed what the amulet itself actually is. He used to be much troubled by a devil, the departed spirit of an east-country Brâhman who died by drowning. He wore the charm to keep this gentleman off.

(4) Aged 24. A silver girdle worn, instead of a string, to which the languti is tied. An iron ring on the 3rd toe of the left foot. Rings are very rarely worn on the toes by any people in Malabar. All over the rest of the Madras Presidency they are, of course, common.

(5) Aged 39. Three earrings, of the usual pattern in each ear. A ring called an elephant's ring, made of silver, in which is arranged circularly a piece of the hair of an elephant's tail, worn on the ring finger of the left hand. There is one of these rings in my collection.

Names, etc., of a few are given—

Taravâd.	Name.	Occupation.	Age.
Pilathottathil ...	Thêyyan Mênon ...	Amshom Mênon or writer. ...	44
Potishêri	Unikkandan ...	Post runner	31
Valia parambath ...	Râman	Peon	20
Chatho Vîtil	Vêlappa Mênon ...	Servant	26
Chandrethil ...	Kuttan	Do.	22
Earat	Krishnan	Cartman	39
Kanjôli	Shangara Mênon ...	Writer in a temple ...	34
Kôlangyarath ...	Chandu	Cooly	36

This last-named individual was measured in the Cannanore Jail, in which institution he, a prisoner himself, filled the office of hangman. He had hanged 10 men in the jail, and, at the rate of 2 rupees a case, he was owed 20 rupees; a nice little sum, which he would be given when leaving the jail at the expiration of his sentence. I was surprised to find a man of the Nâyar caste filling the office of hangman, so enquired the reason and was informed he had put aside the caste scruples while in jail. The office was in its way lucrative, and, when he emerged into freedom, no one would be the wiser, and he would have twenty and odd rupees in his pocket. He did not mind violating certain principles of his caste, doing that which is derogatory, so long as no one knew; but he *did* mind being found out.

KURUP NÂYARS.

The number examined, 8, is not, of course, enough on which to base dependable averages. The men of this clan are—judging by the average such as it is—the tallest of all those examined. Tall, straight, well-bred looking men they are, carrying with them an air of independence and self-respect as one of the old fighting clans. It will be observed that the cephalic length is greater than the average for all the Nâyars, while the cephalic index is less, showing that they are longer headed, and more dolichocephalic than the average Nâyar. Again, the measure of vertex to chin is much greater than in any other clan; and their faces are narrower. The index $\frac{\text{Bizygomatic} \times 100}{\text{Vertex to chin}}$ gives the Nambûtiri one of 69.5, all the Nâyars excluding the Kurups 66.2, and the Kurups 64.5.

The men are called by their clan name, Râma Kurup, Krishna Kurup, Gôvinda Kurup. The name Rama seems to be a favourite one, as four out of eight were so called.

Ages ranging between 20 and 72 *.	Maximum.	Minimum.	Averages of 8.	To stature =100.
Stature	174·9	163·4	167·1	...
Height, sitting	88·8	82·9	85·7	51 3
Do. kneeling	130·3	120·2	124·1	74·3
Span	184·8	173·0	178·6	106·8
Chest	89·4	78·3	82·4	49·3
Shoulders	42·2	38·8	40·4	24·2
Left cubit	51·0	45·1	47·5	28·4
Left hand length	20·8	18·2	19·3	11·5
Do. width	8·8	7·7	8·2	..
Left middle finger	12·3	10·9	11·5	6·9
Hips	28·4	24·5	26·4	15·2
Left foot length	28·0	24·9	26·4	15·2
Do. width	9·5	8·0	8·8	...
Cephalic length	20·6	18·9	19·5	11·7
Do. width	14·6	13·4	14·0	...
Do. index	74·6	68·9	72·0	..
Bigoniac	10·9	9·6	10·3	...
Bizygomatic	13·7	12·3	13·1	...
Maxillo-zygomatic index	83·5	76·7	79·6	...
Nasal length...	5·3	4·4	4·8	2·87
Do. width	3·9	3·4	3·7	...
Do. index	84·1	64·2	76·2	...
Vertex to tragus	14·3	12·3	13·2	7·9
Do. to chin	21·8	19·0	23·3	12·1
Middle finger to patella	13·0	3·6	9·2	5·51

* The man who said he was by his horoscope 72 was put down by me as looking 58.

In two individuals (out of 8) the cephalic length was over 20 cm. In three the nasal height was 5 cm. and over.

Face.—The notes made on two subjects are—

(1) Forehead high. Supraciliary arches distinctly developed. Very deep nasal notch. Nasal point elevated above the line of the nose.

(2) Supraciliary arches not apparent. Nasal point slightly elevated.

Figure.—The greater number are noted as slight; about one-third as medium to stoutly built.

Hair.—Much as those of the other clans. The man who said he was 72, but who looked 58, showed no sign of baldness; his hair was but moderately grey. Another, aged 36, a very strongly-built man, was becoming bald. Baldness at his age is, I should say, rare.

Colour of the skin.—The average is a trifle darker than 29 (Broca). The fairest was fairer than 29, and the darkest was No. 43.

Colour of the eyes.—The average colour of those examined is between 1 and 2 (Broca).

Ornaments call for no remark; they are much as those worn by other Nâyars. Ears are always pierced and earrings worn.

It would be profitless to deal separately with the measures of the individuals comprising the group A in the same way as the others which are more or less complete, with the exception of the Kurup clan. As said already in the group A consists of—

2 of the Nelliôden clan.	3 of the Pallichan clan.
2 ,, Viyyûr clan.	1 ,, Muppattinâyiran clan.
1 ,, Vangilôth clan.	2 ,, Vyâpâri clan.
1 ,, Kitâvu clan.	1 ,, Attikkurissi clan.

and their measures taken collectively have been quoted. The Attikkurissi are endogamous, and the Kitâvu do not wear earrings.

At page 60, Bulletin, Vol. III, No. I, where, speaking of the Nambûtiri Brâhmans, it was said that possibly it may be found that marriage between a brother's daughter and a sister's son may be found to produce the finest issue; to be the best for preservation of the race. This kind of marriage of first cousins, but never of progeny of sisters or of brothers, is in a general way the rule throughout Southern India, and it obtains amongst the endogamous Attikkurissi clan of the Nâyars, who look upon it as the most fitting union.

MARRIAGE.

"The haughty nobles and the vulgar race
Never must join the conjugal embrace."
The Lusiad.

The common assertion that there is no such thing as marriage amongst the Nâyars, so easily accepted in belief that the Government has been persuaded into a commission to examine the question and to pass an edict entitled "The Malabar Marriage Bill" (which happily fell dead, and is extremely unlikely to effect the customs of the Nâyars and others following the Marumakkattâyam law of inheritance), reminds one of the weary disquisition by people who are dull enough to try and prove that Shakespeare's plays were not written by Shakespeare, but by another fellow of the same name. No events of life being so realistic to man as marriage and death (to the individual, to the tribe, to the people) shallowness rather than sturdy hardihood of racial character is perhaps indicated when we find any downright change in the ceremonial of marriage, even though it be but some ephemeral divagation and not properly speaking radical change.

Buchanan, writing in 1800, tells us that Nâyar girls are married before 10, so that they may not be deflowered by nature, but the husband never afterwards cohabits with his wife. It would not be decent. He allows her this and that, and she lives in her mother's house where she may admit a lover of her own or of a higher caste; the lover giving her a small present; never a large one, which would indicate that she was influenced by mercenary motives. He says the young people vie with each other for favour of the other sex, but that, should a Nâyar man have intimacy with a Tîyan (a lower caste) woman, he is put to death and the woman is sold to the Mâppilas! In the case of the *chère amie* being a slave—presumably of the Cheruman or cognate tribes—both are put to death. If this be true, there were forcible means used in those days for preventing intermixture of the people of the higher and lower castes. Buchanan tells us also that in North Malabar, where as a rule the lady lives in his home, the Nâyar or Nambûtiri lover may put her to death, should she be guilty of infidelity; and he may send her home whenever he pleases.

The times have changed things a little: a little only because after all the change is on the surface: it is not radical. Now-a-days, when there is a penal code to deal with persons who kill others, the Nâyar cannot keep a concubine of a caste (not a clan) lower than his own without fear of social ex-communication. The killing, except perhaps now and then *sub rosâ*, is a thing of the past.

The custom which permits the woman to cohabit with a man, her equal or superior in caste, has been alluded to more than once. I will now make some use of the (Government) Report of the Malabar Marriage Commission, published in 1894, which contains much information which is extremely valuable to the anthropologist and the folklorist, and none the worse for being found together with views and opinions with which he cannot agree. One of the points to which the Commission directed special attention was "as to the customs connected with Hindu marriages in Malabar" and the evidence collected respecting these may be accepted as correct, and the delineation of existing custom may be taken as authoritative. Now the custom which permits the man to cohabit with a woman lower in the social scale than himself prohibits the woman from exercising the same liberty. "This is called the rule of *Anulómam* and *Pratilómam*. Dr. Gundert derives *Anulómam* from *anu* = with + *lómam* = *rómam* = the hair: going with the hair or grain. So *Pratilómam* means "going against the hair or grain." According to this usage a Nâyar woman, consorting with a man of a higher caste follows the hair, purifies the blood, and raises the progeny in social estimation. By cohabitation with a man of a lower division (clan) or caste, she is guily of *Pratilómam*; and, if the difference of caste were admittedly great, she would be turned out of her family to prevent the whole family being boycotted."

A corollary of this custom is that a Nambûtiri Brâhman father cannot touch his own children by his Nâyar consort without bathing afterwards to remove the pollution. The children in the Marumakkattâyam family belong, of course, to their mother's family, clan, caste. They are Nâyars, not Nambûtiris; so the Nambûtiri cannot touch them without pollution.

The rule of *Anulómam* and *Pratilómam* appears to be observed with the utmost strictness and thoroughness; one finds it obtaining between members of the same clan inhabiting different parts of the country. Mention of this was made on page 83, where it was said that a woman of any clan of North Malabar may not consort with a man of the same clan name belonging to South Malabar. Following this principle, the man may do so. A woman of South Malabar (inferior), mating with a man of her own clan name of North Malabar (superior), would be following anulomam; but a woman of North Malabar cannot, under pain of being guilty of pratilômam, mate with a man of her own clan name of South Malabar. Alliances between the people of North Malabar and South Malabar seem to be extremely rare; partly, perhaps, because of this custom which is all compulsive, partly because the Nâyar women of North Malabar cannot cross the river which marks the boundary between the two. Nor, as said before, can the Nâyar women of Chirakkal, the northern-most portion of Malabar, cross the river which lies between it and South Canara to the northward. Thus, they cannot go beyond their northern or southern boundaries. The origin of this interdiction to cross the river southwards has been explained to me as emanating from a command of the Kólattiri Rajah in days gone by, when, the Arabs having come to the country about Calicut (South Malabar), there was a chance of the women being seized and taken as wives. An explanation which is somewhat fanciful. The prohibition to cross the river to the northwards is supposed to have originated in much the same way, but I have not noted precisely what it is. Again, men of the Kurup clan of Katattanâd may mate with women of the Nambiyâr clan who live in Kôttayam, but they may not mate with women of the Nambiyâr clan living in Chirakkal. The custom imputing superiority or inferiority to those of a clan inhabiting a certain locality is obscure; it has its counterpart elsewhere in Malabar.

"Except the Nambûtiri, the Nâyar has no other priestly, spiritual or religious instructor; and it is for the gratification of this Bhú-dévan (earth god) that the Sûdra woman, if she has any religious instruction at all, is taught that she was created." We have heard what Hamilton has said about this (see Bulletin, Vol. III, No. I). Though the first portion of this statement is not quite accurate, for we have seen that the priests and religious instructors of the Nâyars are not admitted to be, strictly speaking, Nambûtiris, yet on the whole it is not far wrong, as the Nambûtiri is esteemed as a very exalted person, and he may ply his music among the Nâyar ladies without very much restriction. As remarked before, the custom is one which makes for improvement of the race, bound up as it is with the Marumakkattâyam system, which, guided by the anulômam principle, has fewer hindrances in the way of natural selection than perhaps any other marital custom throughout the world.

The divine commands of Srí Parasu Râma, the imputed originator of the Marumakkattâyam system which is followed by 70 per cent. of the people of Malabar, are supposed to be contained in the Kêrala Mâhâtmyam, a work in Sanskrit verse, written on the ordinary Malabar grantham (palm-leaf book). It purports to be a monologue " addressed by the Rishi Garga to Yudhishthira the eldest of the Pândus." Chapter XLIX relates " how certain celestial damsels were brought from Indra's world by Parasu Râma to satisfy the sexual cravings of the Kêralam Brâhmans, and it relates how Parasu Râma at Vishabhadri (Trichûr), pronounced his commandment to the women (not being of the Brâhman caste) to satisfy the desires of Brâhmans, enjoining on them to put off chastity and the cloth which covered their breasts, and declaring that promiscuous intercourse with three or four men in common was void of the least taint of sin." Unfortunately no scholar has given his opinion as to the time when this was written. Most likely it is not very ancient, and may be attributed to device of the Nambûtiris. But it is respected as authoritative. "One of the foremost Nambûtiris in Malabar in respect of wealth, rank, sanctity and learning," in common with the rest of his clan, relied absolutely on it, and informed the Commission: "The Smiriti says the Sûdras' appointed path to heaven is serving the Brâhmans." "The practice of Brâhmans . . . . . having sexual intercourse with servile (Sûdra) women is in accordance with the Sástras." "If a Brâhman wished to have sexual intercourse with a Sûdra's wife, the Sûdra would be bound to gratify the wish." "A Sûdra cannot be sure of the true parentage of the children born of his wife. Hence the Sûdras cannot follow Makkattâyam"—inheritance in the male line. The Zamorin Maharajah Bahadur informed the Commission that "according to Parasu Râma . . . . chastity should not be observed by non-Brâhman females." Again, the " Ettan Tamburan," one of the senior members of the Zamorin's family, a learned Sanscrit scholar said: " It has been ordained by Parasu Râma that in Kêrala, Marumakkatâyam women need not be chaste;" and he quoted a sloka in proof that there should be no such thing as chastity excepting amongst the Brâhman women. And the Kolatûr Vâriyâr, a great personage: "A woman is not forbidden from consorting with more than one man. For the Marumakkatâyam people, who reckon their descent in the female line, there is no objection to any cohabitation which does not contaminate the female element."

The opinions which have been quoted are those of persons of the highest position, principals of the oldest families, and give expression to the old-fashioned Malabar custom which they would be the last to condemn. But it must not be imagined that the goddess Lubricity reigns supreme in Malabar. It seems perhaps to have been indicated that she does. Such is, however, not the case. It has been said by one whose long acquaintance with Malabar gives him what we may call admitted right to express authoritative opinion, that, "nowhere else is the marriage tie more jealously guarded, and its breaches more savagely avenged." We shall know more of the subject presently, when we have done with all that pertains to formal union between the sexes. As a matter of fact lubricity has no more followers in Malabar than elsewhere.

The ceremonies surrounding marriage and death seem to be those in which human feelings are deepest, and consequently in these, more than in any others, we see relics of a long gone past; much of the ceremonial being now apparently meaningless, and handed on after the manner of all ceremonial, for no obvious purpose, long after the original signification has been forgotten. Amongst all races of the world it is the same. These form perhaps—for the ceremonies connected with death are interwoven with primitive religious ideas—the closest links between our earlier ancestors and ourselves. The institution marriage itself is not easily liable to change or even modification, and thus it is, perhaps, that it, the product of a byegone age, is not always suited to the wants of the age in which it is found. It is rarely up to date. It is invariably blended with superstitions and restraints which people believe they believe; and the relations between the sexes are rarely natural, *i.e.*, rarely free from restraints which are souvenirs of the past, and which are resented in the present. Of course amongst primitive peoples changes in respect of marital connexions, as also in respect of death ceremonies, are imperceptible. They must be very small indeed in even an immense period; and in their case there is not that unsuitability to the time in which they exist, which is apparent amongst those societies more liable to change.

But whatever the reasons may be, the relations between the sexes in Malabar are unusually happy. They seem to be more than commonly natural. The most obvious reason for their being so is that they are less influenced by considerations of property than elsewhere. The desire to maintain property within the family is the curse of all natural relations between the sexes. What strange customs has it not put upon mankind! We have some strange examples of these in Southern India, as when a woman is married to the door-post of the house, and the house owner begets children on her to inherit his property; or when a man marries his child to a woman, and himself begets children on her, and the individual who stands in the position of father may be but a few years older than the son. But we need not look farther than Europe for anomalous customs which inhibit the working of the law of natural selection. Malabar is fairly free from unfortunate customs, and it is perfectly fair to say the marital relation amongst the Nâyars is more than commonly natural.

A description of the ceremonies and formalities connected with the marital connexion will now be attempted. The first of these, described as "most peculiar, distinctive, and unique," is the Tâli-kettu-kalyânam. The details of this ceremony vary in different parts of Malabar, but the ceremony itself, in some form, is essential, and must be performed for every Nâyar girl before she attains puberty. Tâli-kettu-kalyânam means marriage by tying the tali, or ceremony of tying the tâli, a small golden ornament, worn on the neck, the ordinary badge of marriage amongst the Dravidian peoples.

The following account was given by M.R.Ry. K. R. Krishna Menon, retired Sub-Judge, to the Commission:—

"The Tâli-kettu-kalyânam is somewhat analogous to what a Dévadâsi (dancing girl attached to pagodas) of other countries undergoes before she begins her profession. Among royal families, and those of certain Edaprabhûs, a Kshatriya,—and among the Chárna sect, a Nedungádi,—is invited to the girl's house at an auspicious hour appointed for the purpose, and in the presence of friends and castemen ties tâli round her neck, and goes away after receiving a certain fee for his trouble. Among the other sects, the horoscope of the girl is examined along with those of the boys of her Enangan (a recognised member of one's own clan) families, and the boy whose horoscope is found to agree with hers, is marked out as a fit person to tie the tâli, and a day is fixed for the tâli-tying ceremony by the astrologer, and information given to the Káranavan of the boy's family. On the appointed day the boy is invited to a house near that of the girl, where he is fed with his friends by the head of the girl's family. The feast is called 'Ayani Unu,' and the boy is thenceforth called 'Manaválan' or 'Pillai' bridegroom. From the house in which the Manaválan is entertained, a procession is formed, preceded by men with sword and shield shouting a kind of war-cry. In the meantime a procession starts from the girl's house, with similar men and cries, and headed by a member of her taravâd, to meet the other procession, and after meeting the Manaválan, he escorts him to the girl's house. After entering the pandal erected for that purpose, he is conducted to a seat of honour and there his feet are washed by the brother of the girl, who receives a pair of cloths on the occasion. The Manaválan is then taken to the centre of the pandal where bamboo-mats, carpets, and white cloths are spread, and seated there. The brother of the girl then carries her from inside of the house, and after going round the pandal three times, places her at the left side of the Manaválan, and the father of the girl then presents a new cloth tied in a kambli to the pair, and with this new cloth (technically called 'mantravadi') they change their dress. The wife of the Káranavan of the girl's taravâd, if she be of the same caste, then decorates the girl by putting anklets, etc. The Purohita called 'Elayatu' (a low class of Brâhmans) then gives the tali to the Manaválan, and the family astrologer shouts 'Muhurtham' (auspicious hour), and the Manaválan, putting his sword on the lap, ties tali round the girl's neck, who is then required to hold an arrow and a looking-glass in her hand. In rich families a Brâhmini sings certain songs intended to bless the couple. In ordinary families who cannot procure her presence, a certain Nayâr who is versed in songs performs the office. The boy and the girl are then carried by Enangans to a decorated apartment in the inner part of the house, where they are required to remain under a sort of pollution for three days. On the fourth day they bathe in some neighbouring tank or river, holding each other's hands. After changing cloths, they come home preceded by a procession, which varies in importance according to the wealth of the girl's family. Tom-toms and elephants usually form part of the procession, and saffron water is sprinkled. When they come home the doors of the house are all shut, which the Manaválan is required to force open. He then enters the house, and takes his seat in the northern wing thereof. The aunt

PL. XI.

A PALNI PILGRIM, WITH HIS KAVADI.

and other female friends of the girl then approach, and give sweetmeats to the couple. The girl then serves food to the boy, and after taking their meals together from the same leaf, they proceed to the pandal, where a cloth is severed into two parts, and each part given to the Manavâlan and girl separately in the presence of Enangans and other friends. The severing of the cloth is supposed to constitute a divorce."

If, as has been said, the "páttu" sung by the Brâhmani, in "*Rig Vêdaswaram*" is in substitution for the Vêdas sung at the Nambûtiri's wedding—because the Vêdas cannot be used by any but Brâhmans—this part of the ceremonial seems to indicate imitation of the Nambûtiris. The Brâhmani is not however a "Brâhman lady" but merely represents one. In North Malabar she is of the Nambîsan caste.

The ceremony is much more analogous to that obtaining in the Bellary district and round about it, through which women, called Basivis, are, after an initiatory ceremony of devotion to a deity, compelled (under certain conditions) to follow no rule of chastity, but whose children are under no degradation, than to the initiation of the Dêvadâsi in her career of harlotry.* It must be said, however, that the ceremony, more especially as modified by poor people, when the Manavâlan is represented by a clay figure adorned with flowers, the handiwork of the girl's mother, looks very like it. But what demands consideration now is the position of Manavâlan to the bride. Does the ceremony confer on him any of the rights of a husband? There is much diversity of opinion on the point. Some say it does, while some say it does not. It seems certain that, as a rule, there can be no cohabitation between the two as a mere corollary of the tâli-tying ceremony. Should there be three girls in a family, *i.e.*, in the same taravâd house, aged, say, 9, 5 and 3, the ceremony is always done for all three at the same time. The only condition as to age of the girl is that the ceremony must be done before she reaches puberty. The bridegroom (to call him so) is selected after consulting agreement between his horoscope and the girl's. He is seated beside her in the marriage pandal, and he invests her with the tâli. They eat of the same plantain leaf (used as a plate throughout Malabar). They are placed in the same chamber, to go through the fiction

---

* An account of the Basivis, their devotion to deities, etc., by the writer will be found in the "Journal of the Anthropological Society of Bombay," Vol. II., 6 (1891).

of cohabitation; and on the fourth day the bridegroom severs his connection with the girl, symbolising divorce by cutting into two pieces the cloth (called kachai cloth) which she wears. The tearing of the cloth is, however, confined to South Malabar. These are the essentials of the ceremony, an adjunct to which is that, in spite of the divorce, the girl observes death-pollution when her Manavâlan dies. The same Manavâlan may tie the tâli on any number of girls, during the same ceremony or at any other time; and he may be old or young. He is often an elderly holy Brâhman, who receives a small present for his services. The ceremony is always the occasion of feasting and jollification. The girl may remove the tâli if she likes after the fourth day.

In some parts of Malabar there is no doubt that the man who performs the rôle of Manavâlan is considered to have some right to the girl, but in such a case it has been already considered that he is a proper man to enter into Sambandham with her. It will be as well to remark here that almost invariably amongst the inferior races, the aboriginals so to speak of Malabar, girls are married (their marriage is consummated) before puberty. The fuss that was made a few years ago (by the shrieking sisterhood) about the age of consent has had no effect there.

The tâli-tying ceremony having been performed while the girl is yet a child, the next step in the matter of her alliance with a man is the arrangement of the Sambandham. As the rule nothing more than the consent of the girl and of her guardian, the Kâranavan of the family, is necessary. There is no religious formality. The tâli-tying ceremony dispenses with everything of the kind. There is, however, in some parts a tendency now-a-days "to surround the occasion of first cohabitation with a more or less elaborate ceremonial." It is quite an informal affair, arranged by the Kâranavans of the two families. Many a time a young fellow of 22 or 24, answering my question whether he had contracted Sambandham with any one, replied that the head of his family had not yet arranged a Sambandham for him. The wishes of the contracting parties—for in great measure it is a contract—and of the heads of the families practically settle the matter. Should the parties find they are unsuited, they part. There is no dragging on under a bondage intolerable to both.

The following account was given by Mr. Chandu Menon (a Nâyar) to the Commission. He says:—

"The variations of the Sambandham are the Pudamuri, Vastradánam, Uzhamporukkuka, Vítáram Kayaruka, etc., which are local expressions hardly understood beyond the localities in which they are used, but there would be hardly a Malayali who would not readily understand what is meant by *Sambandham tudan guga* (to begin Sambandham). The meaning of this phrase which means "to marry" is understood throughout Kéralam in the same way, and there can be no ambiguity or mistake about it.

"It is thus found that Sambandham is the principal word denoting marriage among Marumakkattayam Nâyars. It will also be found on a close and careful examination of facts, that the principal features of this Sambandham ceremony, all over the Kéralam, are in the main the same. As there are different local names denoting marriage, so there may be found local variations in the performance of the ceremony. But the general features are more or less the same. For instance, the examination, prior to the betrothal, of the horoscopes of the bride and the bridegroom to ascertain whether their stars agree astrologically : the appointment of an auspicious day for the celebration of the ceremony : the usual hours at which the ceremony takes place : the presentation of the *danam* (gifts) to the Brahmans : the sumptuous banquet : the meeting of the bride and the bridegroom,—are features which are invariably found in all well-conducted Sambandhams in all parts of Kéralam alike. But here I would beg to state that I should not be understood as saying that each and every one of the formalities above referred to, are gone through at all Sambandhams among respectable Nâyars, and I would further say that they ought to be gone through at every Sambandham, if the parties wish to marry according to the custom of the country. I would now briefly refer to the local variations to be found in the ceremony of the Sambandham, and also the particular incidents attached to certain forms of Sambandham in South Malabar. I shall describe the Putamuri, or Vastradanam, as celebrated in North Malabar, and then show how the other forms of Sambandham differ from it. Of all the forms of Sambandham I consider the *Pudamuri* form the most solemn and the most fashionable in North Malabar. Of course my description will be borne out by the evidence that is before us. The preliminary ceremony, in every Putamuri, is the examination of the horoscopes of the bride and the bridegroom by an astrologer. This takes place in the house of the bride, in the presence of the relations of the bride and bridegroom. The astrologer, after examination, writes down the results of his calculations on a piece of palmyra leaf, with his opinion as to the fitness or otherwise of the match, and hands it over to the bridegroom's relations. If the horoscopes agree, a day is then and there fixed for the celebration of the marriage. This date is also written down on two pieces of cadjan, one of which is handed over to the bride's Kâranavan, and the other to the bridegroom's relations. The astrologer and the bridegroom's party are then feasted in the bride's house, and the former also receives presents in the shape of money or cloth; and this preliminary ceremony, which is invariably performed at all Putamuris in North Malabar, is called 'Putamuri Kurikkal,' but is unknown in South Malabar.

"Some three or four days prior to the date fixed for the celebration of the Putamuri, the bridegroom visits his Kâranavans and elders in caste to obtain formal leave to marry. The bridegroom on such occasion presents his elders with betel and nuts, and obtains their formal sanction to the wedding. On the day appointed the bridegroom proceeds, after sunset, to the house of the bride, accompanied by a number of his friends. He goes in procession, and is received at the gate of the house by the bride's party, and is conducted with his friends to seats provided in the tekkini, or southern hall of the house. There the bridegroom distributes presents (*danam*) or money gifts to the Brahmans assembled. After this the whole party is treated to a sumptuous banquet. It is now time for the astrologer to appear, and announce the auspicious hour fixed. He does it accordingly, and receives his dues. The bridegroom is then taken by one of his friends to the *padinhatta* or principal room of the house. The bridegroom's party has, of course, brought with them a quantity of new cloths and betel leaves and nuts. The cloths are placed in the western room of the house, called padinhatta, in which all religious and other important household ceremonies are usually performed. This room will be decorated, and turned into a bed-room for the occasion. There will be placed in the room a number of lighted lamps, and *Ashtamangaliam*, which consists of eight articles symbolical of *mangaliam* or marriage. These are rice, paddy, the tender leaves of the cocoanut tree, an arrow, a looking glass, a well washed cloth, burning fire, and a small round wooden box called 'cheppu' made in a particular fashion. These will be found placed on the floor of the room aforesaid as the bridegroom enters it. The bridegroom with his groom's-man enters the room through the eastern door. The bride, dressed in rich cloth and bedecked with jewels, enters the room through the western door, accompanied by her aunt or some other elderly lady of her family. The bride stands facing east with the Ashtamangaliam and lit-up lamps in front of her. The groom's-man then hands over to the bridegroom a few pieces of new cloth, and the bridegroom puts them into the hands of the bride. This being done, the elderly lady who accompanied the bride, sprinkles rice over the lit-up lamps, and the head and shoulders of the bride and the bridegroom, and the bridegroom immediately leaves the room, as he has to perform another duty. At the tekkini or southern hall he now presents his elders and friends with cakes, and betel leaf and nuts. Betel and nuts are also given to all the persons assembled at the place. After the departure of the guests the bridegroom retires to the bed-room with the bride.

"This is an unvarnished account of a 'Putamuri.' Next morning the Vettilakkettu or Salkâram ceremony follows, and the bridegroom's female relations take the bride to the husband's house, where there is a feasting, etc., in honour of the occasion.

"Uzhamporukkuka, or Vídâram Kayaral is a peculiar form of marriage in North Malabar. It will be seen from the description given above, that the Putamuri is necessarily a costly ceremony, and many people generally resort to the less costly ceremony of Uzhamporukkuka or Vídáram Kayaral. The features of this ceremony are to a certain extent the same as Putamuri; but it is celebrated on a smaller scale. There is no cloth-giving ceremony. The toasting is confined to the relations of the married couple. The particular incident attached to this form of marriage is that the husband should visit the wife in her house, and is not permitted to take her to his house, unless and until he celebrates the regular Putamuri ceremony. This rule is strictly adhered to in North Malabar, and instances in which the husband and wife joined by Uzhamporukkuka, or Vídáram Kayaral ceremony, and with grown-up children being the issue of such marriage, undergoing the Putamuri ceremony some 15 or 20 years after Uzhamporukkuka, in order to enable the husband to take the wife to his house, are known to me personally.

"The Sambandham of South Malabar, and the Kidakkorakalyánam of Palghat have all or most of the incidents of Putamuri, except the presenting of the cloths. Here money is substituted for cloths, and the other ceremonies are more or less the same. There is also *Salkáram* ceremony, wanting in South Malabar as the wives are not at once taken to the husband's house after marriage."

But all this formality and ceremonial is not the rule. The Sambandham is always a matter for careful arrangement, in which the wishes of the parties to it are considered, and which it is expected will bring mutual benefit to the two Taravâds concerned.

In South Malabar the girl or woman never lives in her husband's house; she lives on in her own Taravâd house and is there visited by her husband. The ordinary huggermugger, which sometimes stultifies all pleasure in existence, is thus avoided. In North Malabar the woman lives in the house with her husband. A point to be noted in this connection is that, when her husband dies, she must leave his house and return to her own at once, before his body is carried out. According to the Kêrala Mâhâtmyam the women in North Malabar (should) live with but one man at a time.

We still, after the manner of children, confound words with things, so it is not surprising that the unfortunate Commission arrived at the conclusion that the institution of marriage was and is entirely absent from the Marumakkattâyam system. "The parties do not plight troth, and do not call God to witness their union." And so forth. But with this conclusion, suitable enough to the high-flown moralist or to the restless beings who would regardlessly sweep away the long results of time and improve on the process of natural development, imposing fanciful arrangements of their own, the anthropologist cannot at all agree. The Sambandham, a regularly formed, and certainly not haphazard alliance between a man and a woman, having the full sanction of the community, is marriage in every sense of the word. If the tâli-tying ceremony gave the girl free liberty, we might well suspect that the Sambandham followed a ceremony, not a marriage ceremony. But such is by no means the case, for, should the woman who is unmarried, for whom Sambandham has not been arranged, or whose husband, the man with whom she had had Sambandham, is dead—there is no such thing as widowhood,—bear a child, she is disgraced, much as is the Brâhman widow under the same circumstances.

What then is the meaning of the assertions of the exponents of the orthodox view that the woman need not be chaste; and so on? The question is not an easy one to answer, but I think we may say with confidence that this orthodox view has been, in some measure, propounded by the Nambûtiris for their own gratification. I have myself known several tragedies arising out of unfaithfulness, and I believe the old fashioned code of custom admitted the right of the husband to kill his wife's lover if he could, and also to kill his wife. No doubt in a great many cases the pair bound together in Sambandham lead lives ordinarily chaste. I do not, however, think that in actuality such is the rule with either party any more than it is in any other community, and sexual affairs are often treated lightly. With taste and consideration too, Hamilton, who arrived at Calicut in 1702, and spent some twenty odd years on the coast, writes thus in speaking of the Nâyars:——" When the man visits the woman he lays down his arms at the door; but, if there are no arms at the door, any acquaintance may visit her. To visit the house when there are arms at the door, or remove them, is death." Now-a-days a man leaves his shoes outside the door. Equality of the sexes in all sexual matters, the man and woman being on terms of equality, having equal freedom, is certainly an uncommon merit in the Marumakkattâyam system. Either party may terminate the union—even after one night of hymeneal bliss; and those who are unsuited to each other sexually, or in the way of temperament, in fact in any way, may put an end to their union and turn towards other partners. It may be thought that this liberty induced perpetual change, so it is as well to state here that it does nothing of the kind. Mere arbitrary divorce is very rare. Permanent attachment is the rule. The basis of the system seems to be that the Taravâd estate is held in trust for the support of the females and of their descendants in the female line. This trust is placed in the hands of the Kâranavan, the senior male member of the Taravâd who is the legal guardian of every member of it, and whose control of the Taravâd property is absolute. The odd feature in the Marumakkattâyam system is that a man has his nephews about him in the house, and not his sons. He lives in one house, while his wife and family live in another. That is, in South Malabar; in North Malabar they live together.

When we come to consider the degrees of relationship within which marriage is prohibited, we find the rule is that persons descended from a common female ancestor are not at liberty to marry. Those of the same Taravâd can never intermarry; but this prohibition does not of course extend to the children of a brother and a sister, who are naturally of different Taravâds. Again, the principle that "no member of the Taravâd of a deceased wife or husband (is) eligible as the second wife or husband is true only as far as the woman is concerned; for a man may marry a woman of his deceased wife's Taravâd. But he who does this is not in harmony with social sentiment." We find this observance amongst the forest Mûppans of Wynâd. In the case of a man's wife dying, I found that a Mûppan could not take another wife from her family.

The rule does not interfere with union between the children (or their descendants) of a brother and sister such children belonging of course, under the Marumakkattâyam system, to different Taravâds. We have seen already, when speaking of the Nambûtiris, that this rule of marriage between the children of a brother and sister, never between the children of two brothers or two sisters, is general throughout Southern India. It seems to be common, though there are exceptions, to the Brâhmans and the peoples commonly called Dravidian, with most of whom it is the most fitting marital union.

It will be interesting to add here a note on Sambandham as it is amongst the Akattu Chârna, or Akathithaparisha Nâyars (Akattu inside, parisha class),* by one of themselves. The members of this clan being devoted to indoor services, chiefly writing and casting accounts. To those of the sub-clan attached to the Zamorin who were sufficiently capable to earn it, he gave the titular honour "Mênon," to be used as an affix to the name. The title Mênon is in general hereditary, but, be it remarked, many who now use it are not entitled to do so. Properly speaking only those whose investiture by the Zamorin or some other recognized chief is undisputed, they or their descendants (in the female line of course), may use it. Those invested pay a small fee to the Zamorin. A man known to me was invested with the title Mênon in 1895 by the Karimpuzha chief, who in presence of a large assembly said thrice "From this day forward I confer on Krishnan Nâyar the title of Krishna Mênon." Now-a-days be it said, the title Mênon is used by Nâyars of clans other than the Akattu Chârna. Those who belong to the sub-clan who owe Lordship to the Zamorin look to him even now to settle their caste disputes, and for permission to perform the tâlikettu and other important ceremonies. The ceremony to be described is that of this sub-clan.

As the old order changeth giving place to new in the distribution of the honourable affix "Mênon," so too doth it change even in such an important piece of life as marriage, or what under another name means the same thing amongst the Nâyars. It is truly sad to read of celebration of a Sambandham ceremony at Calicut whereat there was cake and wine for the guests, and (shades of all the departed!) a ring for the bride. The departure from national and therefore rational custom, for adoption of that which is neither custom nor cere-

* For this note I am indebted to Mr. C. P. Raman Menon, B.A., a prominent Police official of Calicut.

monial when copied meaninglessly, is surely food for painful reflection.

The ceremony to be described is not one of cake and wine, for the doings of people who have reached that bathos have little interest to the anthropologist, though they may have some to the *observer* of social diversions, but the genuine ceremony as done in orthodox fashion in South Malabar without modern adornment will now be described. My informant says in the first place the man should not enter into Sambandham with a woman until he is 30. Now-a-days, when change is running wild, the man is often much less. In North Malabar, which is much more conservative than the south, it was, however, my experience that Sambandham was rare before 27 on the side of the man. And now continue with the Note.* "The Kâranavan and the women † of his household choose the bride, and communicate their choice to the intending bridegroom through a third party; they may not, dare not speak personally to him in the matter. He approves. The bride's people are informally consulted, and if they agree, the astrologer is sent for and examines the horoscopes of both parties to the intended union. As a matter of course these are found to agree, and the astrologer fixes a day for the Sambandham ceremony. A few days before this takes place two or three women of the bridegroom's house visit the bride, intimating beforehand that they are coming. There they are well treated with food and sweetmeats, and when on the point of leaving they inform the senior female that the bridegroom (naming him) wishes to have Sambandham with—(naming her), and such and such a day is auspicious for the ceremony, the proposal is accepted with pleasure and the party (from the bridegroom's house) returns home."

Preparations for feasting are made in the house of the bride as well as in that of the bridegroom on the appointed day. To the former all relations are invited for the evening, and to the latter a few friends who are much of the same age as the bridegroom (for elders never accompany him) are invited to partake of food at 7 or 8 P.M. and accompany him to the bride's house. After eating they escort him, servants carrying betel leaves (one or two hundred according to the means of the Taravâd),

* Of which what follows is an abstract.

† My correspondent uses the word "Ladies." I prefer women, a finer word.

arecanuts and tobacco, to be given to the bride's household, and which are distributed to the guests. When the bride's house is far away the bridegroom makes his procession thither from a neighbouring house. Arrived at the bride's house they sit a while and are again served with food, after which they are conducted to a room where betel and other chewing stuff is placed on brass or silver plates (called thâlam). The chewing over, sweetmeats are served, and then all go to the bridal chamber, where the women of the house and others are assembled with the bride, who, overcome with shyness, hides herself behind the others. Here again the bridegroom and his party go through more chewing while they chat with the women. After a while the men withdraw, wishing the couple all happiness; and then the women, departing one by one leave the couple alone, one of them shutting the door from the outside.

"The Patter Brâhmans always collect on these occasions and receive small presents (dakshina) of 2 to 4 annas each, with betel leaf and areca nut from the bridegroom, sometimes from the bride. A few who are invited receive their dakshina in the bridal chamber; the others outside. [In a Nâyar house the sleeping rooms of the men and women are separate; at different ends of the house.] Those of the bridegroom's party who live far away are given sleeping accommodation at the bride's house, with the men. About daybreak next morning the bridegroom leaves the house with his party, leaving under his pillow Rs. 8, 16, 32 or 64, according to his means but never more than 64, which are intended to cover the expenses of the wife's household on the ceremony. The Sambandham is now complete. The girl remains in her own Taravâd house, and her husband visits her there, coming in the evening and leaving the next morning. A few days after completion of the ceremony the senior woman of the bridegroom's house sends some cloths, including pavu mundu (superior cloths) and thorthu mundu (towels) and some oil to the bride for her use for six months. Every six months she does the same, and on festivals of the Ônam, Vishu, Thiruvathîra she sends besides a little money, areca nut, betel nut and tobacco. The money sent should amount to Rs. 4, or 8, or 16, or 32, or 64; either one of these sums. Sums of the higher numbers are very rarely sent.

"Before long the women of the husband's house express a longing for the girl-wife to be brought to their house, for they have not seen her yet. Again the astrologer is requisitioned, and, on the day he fixes, two or three of the women go to the house of the girl-wife, the Ammâyi as they call her (literally "uncle's wife"). They are well treated, and presently bring away the girl with them. As she is about to enter the gate house of her husband's Taravâd, the stile of which she crosses right leg first, two or three of the women meet her, bearing a burning lamp and a brass plate (tâlam) and precede her to the nalukattu of the house. There she is seated on a mat, and a burning lamp and a nazhi (1 measure) of rice and some plantains are placed before her. One of the younger women [married or not I cannot say] takes up a plantain and puts a piece of it in the Ammâyi's mouth; a little ceremony called Madhuram Tîtal, or giving the sweets for eating. She lives in her husband's house for a few days and is then sent back to her own with presents, bracelets, rings or cloths, gifts of the senior women of the house. After this she is at liberty to visit her husband's house on any day, auspicious or inauspicious.

"In a big Taravâd, where there are many women, the Ammâyi does not, as a rule, disperse sympathy and good will in the household, and if she happens to live temporarily in her husband's house, as is sometimes though very rarely the case in south Malabar, and to be the wife of the Kâranavan, it is observed that she gets, more than her share of whatever good things may be going; hence the proverb 'Ammâyi Ammayê Kallinmel Vechchittu Mattoru Kallu Kondu Nârâyana'—'Place Ammâyi Amma on a stone and grind her with another stone.'"

Yet one more extract—a reference taken from my notes. The Rev. S. Mateer, author of a well-known book on Travancore, where he resided something over a quarter of a century, I think, informed me ten years ago—he was speaking of polyandry amongst the Nâyars of Travancore—that he had "known an instance of 6 brothers keeping 2 women, 4 husbands to one, and 2 to the other. In a case where 2 brothers cohabited with one woman and one was converted to Christianity, the other brother was indignant at the Christian's refusal to live any longer in this condition." I have not known an admitted instance of polyandry amongst the Nâyars of Malabar at the present day, but there is no doubt that if it does not exist now (and I think it does here and there), it certainly did not long ago. Polyandry exists amongst other castes, as we shall see by and by.

We must now leave the subject of marriage, which, simple though it is, is like most simple things extremely difficult to describe. The marital relation of the Nâyar is a very natural and simple affair; yet it is the *point d'appuis* of that system of inheritance through women which was once much more common than it is now.

Let us hope it will remain unchanged, and that the Nâyar will be able to say always (in his own tongue), with more regard for concrete truth than poetic insight "Das ewig' weibliche ziet uns hinan."

BIRTH: ANTE-NATAL AND AFTER CEREMONIES.

The following very interesting note on the ceremonies connected with birth, those preceding it as well as those following it, has been very kindly given by Mr. U. Balakrishnan Nâyar; so I quote his own words:—

"A Nâyar woman has to observe certain ceremonies during pregnancy. First, during and after the seventh month of pregnancy, she (at least, among the well-to-do class) bathes, and worships in the temple, every morning; and eats before her morning meal, a small quantity of butter over which holy *mantrams* have been said by the temple priest or by Nambûtiris. This is generally done till delivery.

"*Puli-kuti.*—Another and even more important ceremony during pregnancy is the *puli-kuti* (lit., drinking tamarind juice). This is an indispensable ceremony, performed by the rich and poor alike, on a particular day in the ninth month. The day, nay, even the very hour is fixed by the local astrologer. The ceremony begins by the planting of a twig of the *ampasham* tree, on the morning of the day of the ceremony, in the principal courtyard *(natu-muttom)* of the *Taravâd.* At the appointed hour or *muhurtam*, the pregnant woman, after having bathed and properly attired, is conducted to a particular portion of the house (*vatakini* or northern wing), where she is seated, facing eastwards. The *Ammâyi* or 'uncle's wife,' whose presence on the occasion is essential, goes to the courtyard and plucking a few leaves of the planted twig, squeezes a few drops of its juice into a cup. This she hands over to the brother, if any, of the pregnant woman. It is necessary that the brother should wear a gold ring on his right-hand ring finger. Holding a

PL. XII.

A VELICHCHAPPAD.

country knife *(pissan kathi)* in his left hand, which he directs towards the mouth, he pours the tamarind juice over this knife with his right hand three times, which dribbles down the knife into her mouth, and she drinks it. In the absence of a brother, some other near relation officiates. After she has swallowed the tamarind juice, she is asked to pick one out of several packets of different grains placed before her. The grain in the packet she happens to select is supposed to declare the sex of the child in her womb. The whole ceremony is wound up by a sumptuous feast to all the relatives and friends of the family.

"*After Ceremonies.*—At delivery, women of the barber caste officiate as midwives. In some localities, this duty is performed by *Vêla* caste women. Pollution is observed for fifteen days, and on every day, the mother wears cloths washed and presented her by a *Vannatti* or woman of the Vannan * caste. On the fifteenth day is the purificatory ceremony. As in the case of death pollution, a man of the Atikkurissi clan sprinkles on the woman a liquid mixture of oil, and the five products of the cow (*pancha gavya*), with gingelly seeds. Then the woman takes a plunge-bath and sits on the ground, near the tank or river. Some woman of the family, with a copper vessel in her hands, takes water out of the tank or river, and pours it on the mother's head as many as twenty-one times. (I am not aware if this practice is universal, though it certainly obtains in parts of South Malabar and even in North Travancore.) This done, she again plunges herself in the tank or river, from which she emerges thoroughly purified.

"It may be noticed that, before the mother proceeds to purify herself, the new-born babe has also to undergo some rite of purification. The babe is placed on the naked floor, and its father or uncle sprinkles a few drops of cold water on it and takes it in his hands. The superstitious believe that the temperament of the child is determined by that of the person who thus sprinkles the water. All members of the *Taravâd* observe pollution for fifteen days immediately following the delivery, during which period they are prohibited from entering temples and holy places.

"*First Birthday Celebration.*—The twenty-seventh day after the child's birth or the first recurring day of the star under which it was born marks the next important

* Over a great part of Malabar she would, however, be of the Tiyan caste.

event. On this day, the *Kârnavan* of the family gives to the child a spoonful or two of milk, mixed with sugar and slices of plantain. Then he names the child and calls it in the ear by the name* three times. This is followed by a feast to all friends and relatives, the expenses of which are necessarily met by the father of the child.

" *Chôrûn or First Meal of Rice.*—As is usual with the Nâyar every event is introduced by a ceremonial. The first meal of rice partaken by the child forms no exception to the rule. It must be remembered that the child is not fed on rice for some time after birth; the practice being to give it flour of dried plantain boiled with jaggery. There is a particular variety of plantain, known as *kunnan*, used for this purpose. The staple food of the Malayali, rice, is given the child, for the first time, generally during the sixth month, and is attended, of course, with some ceremonial. Necessarily, the astrologer fixes the day; and at the auspicious hour, the child, bathed and adorned with ornaments (which it is the duty of the father to provide) is brought and laid on a plank. A plantain-leaf is spread in front of it and a lighted brass lamp, placed near. On the leaf are† served a small quantity of cooked rice—generally a portion of the rice offered to some temple divinity—some tamarind, salt, chillies, and sugar. Then the *Kâranavan* or the father, ceremoniously approaches and sits down facing the child. First, he puts in the mouth of the child a mixture of the tamarind, chillies and salt; then some rice; and lastly a little sugar.

"Thenceforward, the ordinary food of the child is rice. It is usual on this occasion for relatives (and especially for the '*bandhus*,' such as the *Ammâyi* or 'uncle's wife') to adorn the child with gold bangles, rings and other ornaments. The *chôrûnû* or rice-giving ceremony is, in some cases, preferably performed in some famous temple, that at Guruváyûr being a favourite one for this purpose.

" *Child-birth—Position during.*—When a Nâyar woman is about to be delivered of a child, she is placed in a reclining position on a low wooden couch (Kottotam), her back supported by a companion, generally an old woman. The kottotam is very like, if not identical with,

---

* In some places, the child is named only in the sixth month on the chôrûn day.

† In some places, all the curries, etc., prepared for the attendant feast are also served.

the couch on which the Nâyar has his oil bath. The surface of it is sloping, the higher end being where the head is laid, and it is scooped out so as to suit the curvatures of the body lying flat.* Lying on her back, her head is raised and the thighs are stretched wide apart. Very often she holds in each hand a rope suspended from the ceiling, by way of support. The child is received by a woman of the barber caste."

DEATH AND SUCCEEDING CEREMONIES.

When the dying person is about to embark for that bourne from which no traveller returns, when the breath is about to leave his body, the members of the household, and all friends who may be present, one by one pour a little water, a few drops from a tiny cup made of a leaf or two of the tulsi plant, into his mouth, holding in the hand a piece of gold or a gold ring; the idea being that the water should touch gold ere it enters the mouth of the person who is dying. If the Taravâd is rich enough to afford it, a small gold coin, (a Râsi fanam, if one can be procured †) is placed in the mouth, and the lips are closed. As soon as death has taken place, the corpse is removed from the cot or bed, and carried to the vatakkini (a room in the northern end of the house) where it is placed on long plantain leaves spread out on the floor; and while it is in this room, whether by day or by night, a lamp is kept burning, and one member of the Taravâd holds the head in his lap and another the feet in the same way; and here the neighbours come to take a farewell look at the dead.

As the Malayâlis believe that disposal of a corpse by cremation or burial as soon as possible after death is conducive to the happiness of the spirit of the departed, no time is lost in setting about the funeral. The bodies of senior members of a Taravâd, male or female, are burned; those of children under two are buried; so too are the bodies of all persons who have died of cholera or smallpox.‡ When preparations for the funeral have been made, the corpse is removed to the natumuttam or central yard of the house if there is one (there always is

---

* Every Nâyar, and for the matter of that, every Malayali, has an oil bath about once a week or as often as he can afford. The person is well shampooed with gingelly oil.

† These are now rare.

‡ It is the same amongst the Khonds of Ganjam.

in the larger houses), and, if there is not, is taken to the front yard where it is again laid on plantain leaves. It is washed and anointed, the usual marks are made with sandalwood paste and ashes as in life, and it is neatly clothed. There is then done what is called the Pota-vekkuka ceremony or placing new cotton cloths (kóti mundu) over the corpse by the senior member of the (deceased's) Taravâd followed by all the other members, also sons-in-law and daughters-in-law, and all relatives. These cloths are used for tying up the corpse when being taken to the place of burial or cremation. In some parts of Malabar the corpse is carried on a bier made of fresh bamboos, tied up in these cloths, while in others it is carried (well covered in the cloths) by hand. In either case it is carried by the relatives. Before the corpse is removed there is done another ceremony called Para Virakkuka (filling up pâras—a pâra is a measure nearly as big as a gallon). All adult male members of the Taravâd take part in it under the direction of a man of the Atikkurissi clan (who occupies the position of director of the ceremonies during the next fifteen days, receiving as his perquisite all the rice and other offerings made to the deceased's spirit). It consists in filling up three pâra measures with paddy, and one edangâli ($\frac{1}{10}$ of a pâra) with raw rice. These offerings of paddy and rice are placed very near the corpse, together with a (burning) lamp of the kind commonly used in Malabar, called nela villâku. If the Taravâd is rich enough to afford one, a silk cloth is placed over the corpse before removal for cremation.

As much fuel as is necessary having been got ready at the place of cremation, a small pit about the size of the corpse is dug, and across this are placed three long stumps of the plantain tree, one at each end, one in the middle; on which as a foundation the pyre is laid. The whole, or at least a part of the wood used should be that of the mango tree. As the corpse is being removed to the pyre, the senior Anandravan * who is next in age (junior) to the deceased, tears from one of the new cloths laid on the corpse a piece sufficient to go round his waist, ties it round his waist, and holds in his hand, or tucks into his cloth at the waist a piece of iron, generally a

* The eldest male member of the Malabar Taravâd is called the Kâranavan, as noted already (Bulletin, Vol. III, No. 1); all male members, brothers, nephews and so on, who are junior to him are called Anandravans of the Taravâd.

long key. This individual is throughout *chief* among the offerers of "pindam" (balls of rice) to the deceased.

The corpse is laid on the bier, with the head to the south, with the fuel laid over it and a little camphor, sandalwood and ghee, if these things are within the means of the Taravâd. Here must be stated the invariable rule that no member of the Taravâd, male or female, who is older than the deceased shall take any part whatever in the ceremony, or in any subsequent ceremony following on the cremation or burial. All adult males junior to the deceased should be present when the pyre is lighted. The deceased's younger brother, or, if there is none surviving, his nephew (his sister's eldest son), sets fire to the pyre at the head of the corpse. If the deceased left a son, this son sets fire at the same time to the pyre at the feet of the corpse. In the case of the deceased being a woman, her son sets fire to the pyre; failing a son the next (junior) in age to her has the right to do it. It is a matter of great importance that the whole pyre burns at once: the greatest care is taken that it burns as a whole, consuming every part of the corpse. While the corpse is being consumed, all the members of the deceased's Taravâd who carried it to the pyre go and bathe in a tank (there is always one in the compound or garden around every Nâyar's house): the eldest, he who bears the piece of torn cloth and the piece of iron (the key), carries an earthen pot of water, and all return together to the place of cremation. It should be said that on the news of a death the neighbours assemble, assisting in digging the grave, preparing the pyre, and so on, and, while the members of the Taravâd go and bathe, those remain near the corpse. By the time the relatives return it is almost consumed by the fire, and the senior Anandravan carries the pot of water thrice round the pyre, letting the water leak out by making holes in the pot as he walks round. On completing the third round, he dashes the pot on the ground close by where the head of the dead had been placed. A small image of the deceased is then made out of raw rice * representing the deceased, and to this image a few grains of rice and gingelly seeds are offered. When this has been done the relatives go home and the neighbours depart, bathing before entering their houses.

* The ceremony is called Veli Unka (?).

When the cremation has been done by night, the duty of Sêshakriya (making offerings to the deceased's spirit) must be begun the next day between 10 and 11 A.M. and is done on seven consecutive days. In any case the time for this ceremony is after 10 and before 11 and it continues for seven days. It is performed as follows. All male members of the Taravâd younger than the deceased go together to a tank and bathe, *i.e.*, they souse themselves in the water, and return to the house. The eldest of them, the man who tore off the strip of cloth from the corpse, has with him the same strip of cloth and the piece of iron, and all assemble in the central courtyard of the house, where there has been placed ready by an Enangan—(one of the Taravâd—of the same clan or sub-clan as that of the deceased : marriage must be admissible between the two Taravâds)—some rice which has been half boiled, a few grains of gingelly, a few leaves of the cherûla,* some curds, a smaller measure † of paddy, and a smaller measure ‡ of raw rice. These are placed in the north-east corner with a lamp of the ordinary Malabar pattern. A piece of palmyra leaf, about a foot or so in length and the width of a finger, is taken, and one end of it knotted ; the knotted end is placed in the ground, and the long end is left sticking up. This represents the deceased. The rice and other things are offered to this. The belief concerning this piece of palmyra leaf is explained thus : There are in the human body ten humours :—Vâyús ; Prânan ; Apânan ; Samânan ; Udânan; Vyânan ; Nâgan ; Kûrman; Krikalan ; Dêvadattan ; Dhananjayan. These are called Dasaváyu, *i.e.*, ten airs. When cremation was done for the first time, all these excepting the last, were destroyed by the fire. The last one flew up and settled on a palmyra leaf. Its existence was discovered by some Brâhman sages who, by means of mantrams (magic), forced it down to a piece of palmyra leaf on the earth. So it is thought that, by making offerings to this (Dhananjayan) leaf for seven days, the spirit of the deceased will be mollified, should he have any anger to vent on the living members of the Taravâd.

The place where the piece of leaf is to be fixed has been cleaned carefully, and the leaf is fixed in the centre of this prepared surface. The offerings made to it go direct

---

* Ærna lanata belonging to the natural order Acanthaceæ.

† An Edangâli : about the size of a quart.

‡ A nazhi : about ½ a pint.

to the spirit of the deceased, and the peace of theTaravâd is ensured. The men who have bathed and returned have brought with them, plucked on their way back to the house, some grass (karuka pullu): they kneel in front of the piece of palmyra, with the right knee on the ground. Some of the grass is spread on the ground near the piece of leaf, and rings made with it are placed on the ring finger of the right hand by each one present. The first offerings consist of water, sandalwood paste and leaves of the cherîla : the eldest of the Anandravans leading the way. Boys need not go through the actual performance of offerings ; it suffices for them to touch the eldest as he is making his offerings. The half-boiled rice is made into balls (pindams) and each one present takes one of these in his right hand and places it on the grass near the piece of palmyra leaf. Some gingelly seeds are put into the curd, which is poured so as to make three rings round the pindams. It is poured out of a small cup made with the leaf on which the half-boiled rice had been placed. It should not be poured from any other kind of vessel. The whole is then covered with this same plantain leaf, some lighted wick is waved, and some milk is put under the leaf. It is undisturbed for some moments, and the leaf is tapped gently with the back of the fingers of the right hand. The leaf is then removed and torn in two at its midrib, one piece being placed on either side of the pindams. The ceremony is then over for the day. The performers rise, and remove the wet clothing they have been wearing.

The eldest of the Anandravans should, it was omitted to mention, be kept somewhat separated from the other Anandravans while in the courtyard, andbefore the corpse is removed for cremation ; a son-in-law or a daughter-in-law, or some such kind of relation remaining, as it were, between him and them. He has had the piece of cloth torn from the covering of the corpse tied round his waist, and he has had the piece of iron (usually a key) in the folds of his cloth, or stuck in his waist during the ceremony which has just been described. Now, when it has been completed, he ties the piece of cloth to the pillar of the house nearest to the piece of palmyra leaf which has been stuck in the ground, and puts the piece of iron in a safe place. The piece of palmyra leaf is covered with a basket. It is uncovered every day for seven days at the same hour, while the same ceremony is repeated. The balls of rice (pindams) are removed by women and girls of the Taravâd who are junior to the deceased. They place them in the bell-metal vessel in which the rice was boiled. The senior places the vessel on her head, and leads the way to a tank, on the banks of which the rice is thrown. It is hoped that crows will come and eat it; for if they do, the impression is received that the deceased's spirit is pleased with the offering; but if somehow it is thought that the crows will not come and eat it, the rice is thrown into the tank. Dogs are not to be allowed to eat it. The women bathe after the rice has been thrown away.

When the ceremony which has been described has been performed for the seventh time, *i.e.*, on the seventh day after death, the piece of palmyra leaf is removed from the ground, and thrown on the ashes of the deceased at the place of cremation. During these seven days no member of the Taravâd goes to any other house. The house of the dead and all its inmates are under pollution : no outsider enters it but under ban of pollution, which is, however, removable by bathing. A visitor entering the house of the dead during these seven days must bathe before he can enter his own house. During these seven days the Kâranavan of the family receives visits of condolence from relatives and friends to whom he is "at home" on Monday, Wednesday or Saturday. They sit and chat, chew betel and go home, bathing ere they enter their houses.

It is said that in some parts of Malabar the visitors bring with them small presents in money or kind to help the Kâranavan through the expenditure to which the funeral rites necessarily put him.

To hark back a little, it must not be omitted that on the third day after the death, all those who are related by marriage to the Taravâd of the deceased combine and give a good feast to the inmates of the house and to the neighbours, who are invited, one man or one woman from each house. The person so invited is expected to come. This feast is called Patni Karigi. On the seventh day a return feast will be given by the Taravâd of the deceased to all relatives and neighbours.

Between the seventh and fourteenth day after death no ceremony is observed ; but the members of the Taravâd remain under death pollution, and then on the fourteenth day comes the Sanchayanam. It is the disposal of the calcined remains ; the ashes of the deceased. The male members of the Taravâd go to the place of cremation and, picking up the pieces of unburnt bones which they find there, place these in an earthen pot which has been sun-dried—not burnt by fire in the usual way—cover up the mouth of this pot with a piece of new cloth, and, all following the eldest who carries it, proceed to the nearest river (it must be running water), which receives the remains of the dead. The men then bathe and return home. In some parts of Malabar the bones are collected on the seventh day, but it is not orthodox to do so. Better by far than taking the remains to the nearest river is it to take them to some specially sacred place, Benares, Gâya, Ramêsvaram, or even to some place of sanctity much nearer home, as to Tirunelli in Wynâd, and there dispose of them in the same manner. The bones or ashes of any one having been taken to Gâya and there deposited in the river, the survivors of the Taravâd have no need to continue the annual ceremony for that person. This is called "Ashtagâya Shraddham." It puts an end to the need for all earthly ceremonial. It is believed that the collection and careful disposal of the ashes of the dead gives peace to his spirit, and, what is more important, the pacified spirit will not thereafter injure the living members of the Taravâd, cause miscarriage to the women, possess the men (as with an evil spirit), and so on.

Then on the fifteenth day after death is the purificatory ceremony. Until this has been done, any one touched by any member of the Taravâd should bathe before he enters his house or partakes of any food. A man of the Athikkurisi clan officiates. He sprinkles milk oil in which have been put some gingelly seeds (all together) over the persons of those under pollution. This sprinkling and the bath which follows it removes the death pollution. The purifier receives a fixed remuneration for his office on this occasion, as well as when there is a birth in the Taravâd.

In the case of death of a senior member of a Taravâd, well-to-do and reckoned as of some importance, there is the feast called Pinda Atiyantaram on the sixteenth day after death, given to the neighbours and friends. The word neighbours, as used here, does not mean those who live close by, but, owing to the custom of Malabar under which each house is in its own paramba (garden or enclosure) which may be a large one, those of the caste living within a considerable area round about. I am not sure whether in connection with these ceremonies there is mutual assistance in preparation for the funeral; or whether there is any recognized obligation between members of the same amsham, dêsam or tara; or whether this kind of mutual obligation obtains generally between any Taravâd and those of caste round about, irrespective of boundaries. With the observance of the Pinda Atiyantaram or feast of pindams, there is involved the Dîkṣha, or leaving the entire body unshaved for 41 days, or for a year. There is no variable limit between 41 days or a year. Forty-one days is permissible as the period for the Dîkṣha, but a year is correct. The 41-day period is the rule in North Malabar.

I have seen many who were under the Dîkṣha for a year. He who lets his hair grow may be a son or nephew of the deceased. One member only of the Taravâd bears the mark of mourning by his growth of hair, remarkable enough in Malabar where every one as a rule, excepting the Mâppila Muhammadans (and they shave their heads), shaves his face, head (except the patch on the crown) chest and arms, or at any rate his wrists. He who is under the Dîkṣha offers half-boiled rice and gingelly seeds to the spirit of the decased every morning after his bath; and he is under restriction from women, from alchoholic drinks, and from chewing betel, also tobacco. When the Dîkṣha is observed, the ashes of the dead are not deposited as described already (in the sun-dried vessel) until its last day—the forty-first or a year after death. When it is carried on for a year there is observed every month a ceremony called * Bali. It is noteworthy that, in this monthly ceremony and for the conclusion of the Dîkṣha, it is not the thirtieth or three hundred and sixty-fifth day which marks the date for the ceremonies, but it is the day (of the month) of the star which was presiding when the deceased met his death: the returning day on which the star presides.

For the * Bali, a man of the Elâyatu caste officiates. It has been said already ("Nambûtiri Brâhmans": Bulletin, Vol. III, No. I), that the Elâyatus are priests for the Nâyars. They wear the Brâhman's thread, but they are not Brâhmans. They are not permitted to study the Vêdas, but to the Nâyars they stand in the place of the ordinary Purôhit. The officiating Elâyatu prepares the rice for the Vêli when the deceased, represented by Karuka grass, is offered boiled rice, curds, gingelly seeds and some other things. The Elâyatu should be paid a rupee for his services, which are considered necessary even when the man under Dîkṣha himself is familiar with the required ceremonial.

The last day of the Dîkṣha is one of festivity. After the * Bali the man under Dîkṣha is shaved. All this over

* Or Bâli.

BHAGAVATI TEMPLE, PANDALUR.

the only thing to be done for the deceased is the annual shraddham, or yearly funeral commemorative rite. Rice balls (pindams) are made and given to crows. Clapping of hands announces to these birds that the rice is being thrown for them, and, should they come at once and eat it, it is obvious that the spirit of the deceased is pleased with the offering, and is not likely to be troublesome. But, on the other hand, should they not come and eat, it is evident that the spirit is displeased, and the Taravâd had better look out.

The ceremonial connected with the funeral rites which have been described, illustrates the immense difference which exists, as it does in the case of all peoples more or less cultured, between the primitive belief of the race, and the higher, the more abstract, religion which they believe they believe. With races, as with children, the earliest associations are the strongest, and persist through the life of the race as through the life of the individual. The higher power of reasoning which comes with higher development does not disperse them altogether. The people who practise these rites are good Hindus, and, according to the theory of their Hindu religion, the spirit which is emancipated from the body at death at once inhabits another body, for suffering or for enjoyment measured by the deserts of the bodily existence which has just ceased. This is the higher religion. And yet they admit that the spirit is connected with the shadow, not with the breath;—and feel in their hearts that it still lingers in the house and absorbs the essence of the ingredients of the food offered to it; that it must be propitiated or it will cause harm to the living. This is the primitive religion. It is supposed that the spirits of those whose ashes are deposited at Benares or other place of sanctity, and for whose sake alms are given to Brâhmans, remain at those holy spots, and become more and more god-like. This is a mixture of both. We are here concerned with facts rather than theories and, as much has been said already of this side of the subject of comparative religions, we may proceed with our facts. The spirits of those who have committed suicide or met death by any violent means are always particularly vicious and troublesome to the Taravâd, their spirit possessing and rendering miserable some unfortunate member of it. Unless pacified they will ruin the Taravâd, so Brâhman priests are called in and appease them by means of Tilahômam, a rite in which sacrifical fire is raised, and ghee, gingelly and other things are offered through it.

RELIGION.

It will be easier to convey a rational conception of the religion of the Nâyars, not by what is written but by what is left out; so we will proceed on this plan. The ceremonies connected with marriage and death go far towards indicating what are their religious ideas in general. The conservative character of the people of Malabar whose country is an earthly paradise, severed from the major portion of the Indian peninsula by the high mountains of the Western Ghâts, secure in its happy seclusion, where Nature has lavished her gifts with the prodigality of a Bacchante, prepares us for finding much of the primitive element in their religion. With the more uncultivated, the wilder races, this is almost entirely primitive in character; no more the cult of a Siva or Vishnu than of Sqaktktquaclt.

As has been remarked already ("Nambûtiris" Bulletin, Vol. III, No. I), we see in Malabar the most undiluted form of the highest, the most abstract religion of Southern India, side by side with the most entirely primitive. The Nâyars have much of both.

The saying, "cleanliness is next to godliness," is one of those which contain much more real wisdom than is usually apprehended. The world is really divided, as I think Mr. Havelock Ellis points out, between the dirty and the clean; and, if I err not, the same author tells us that clothed man cannot be truly clean. Man has advanced far in development when he has become a clean animal. Now the Nâyars' religion is one of cleanliness, undiminished by superabundant clothing. Men and women can scarcely wear less than they do in compatibility with the received ideas of decency and propriety, nor can they be more scrupulous in the matter of personal cleanliness. No Nâyar, unless one utterly degraded by the exigencies of a Government office, would eat his food without having bathed and changed his cloth. It is a rule seldom broken that every Nâyar goes to the temple to pray at least once a day after having bathed; generally twice a day. The mere approach anywhere near his vicinity of a Cheruman, a Polayan or any inferior being, even a Tîyan, as he walks to his house from the temple, cleansed in body and mind, his marks newly set on his forehead with sandalwood paste, is pollution, and he must turn and bathe again ere he can enter his house and eat. Buchanan tells us that in his time, about 99 years ago, the man of inferior caste thus approaching the Nâyar would be cut down instantly with a sword: there would be no words. Now that the people of India are inconvenienced with an Arms Act which inhibits sword play of this kind, and with a law-system under which high and low are rated alike, the Nâyar has to content himself with an imperious grunt-like shout for the way to be cleared for him as he stalks on unperturbed. His arrogance is not diminished, but he cannot now show it in quite the same way.

Doubtless the natural habit of seclusion common to Malabar, rendered easy by the wealth of vegetation of which those who have never visited shores somewhat alike climatically can have no conception, has favoured the persistence of earlier forms of belief; but, whatever may be the reason for it, there is much more of the extremes of religious belief to be seen amongst the Nâyars than amongst any other people or caste of Southern India.

It has been noticed already how that the Malayalis have, practically, no sects such as obtain throughout the rest of Southern India. Vishnu, Siva, Bhagavati, Rama—all these names of the Hindu theogony are meaningless to them. They do not know one from the other except in name. Their Hinduism is not that of the rest of Southern India.

It is time to come to concrete example, so I will attempt a description of the ceremonial observed at the Pishâri kâvu—the Pishâri temple near Quilandy on the coast 15 miles north of Calicut, where Bhagavati is supposed in vague legend to have slain an Asura or gigantic ogre, in commemoration of which event the festival is held yearly to Bhagavati and her followers. It is fairly representative. The deity of the temple Bhagavati is spoken of as feminine in the spirit of accuracy, but it is extremely unlikely whether ten per cent. of the crowd even thought of sex in connection with Bhagavati. Sacrifice of goats as part of the ceremonial was at first denied: it is a mystery too awful to be the subject of conversation. At the same time, I am inclined to think that much the weighter reason is that the priests who cling to this part of the ceremonial are ashamed to let it be known to the people that they do it. They like it to be thought that such sacrifice is appropriate to the inferior races, but that *they* are above it and have nothing to do with it!

The festival lasts for seven days. When I visited it in 1895 the last day was on the 31st of March. Before day-break of the first day the ordinary temple priests, a Mûssad, will leave the temple after having swept up and made it clean; and (before day-break also) five Nambûtiris will enter it, bearing with them "Sudhi Kalasam." The Kalasam is on this occasion made of the five products of the cow, *i.e.* (panchagavyam) together with some water, a few leaves of the banyan tree (Arayâl) and Darbha grass, all in one vessel. Before being brought to the temple, mantrams or magic verses will have been said over it. The contents of the vessel are sprinkled all about the temple, and a little is put in the well, thus purifying the temple and the well. The Nambûtiris will then perform the usual morning worship, and either immediately after it or very soon afterwards they leave the temple, and the Mûssad, the ordinary priest, returns and resumes his office. The temple belongs to four Taravâds, and no sooner has it been purified than the Kâranavans of these four Taravâds, virtually the joint-owners of the temple (known as Urâlas) present to the temple servant (known as a Pishârodi) the silver flag of the temple which has been in the custody of one of them since the last festival. The Pishârodi receives it and hoists it in front of the temple (to the east), thus signifying that the festival has begun. While this is being done, emphasis and grandeur is given to the occasion by the firing off of miniature mortars such as are common at all South Indian festivals; and, after the flag is hoisted, there are hoisted all round the temple small flags of coloured cloth. For the next few days there is nothing particular to be done beyond the procession morning, noon and night; the image of Bhagavati being carried on an elephant to an orchestra of drums, and cannonade of the little mortars. All those who are present are supposed to be fed from the temple. There is a large crowd. On the morning of the fifth day a man of the washerman (he is also a tailor: Vannân) caste will announce to the neighbours by beat of tom-tom that there will be made a procession of Bhagavati issuing from the gates of the temple and passing round about. Like all those who are in any way connected with the temple, this man's office is hereditary and he lives to a small extent on the bounty of the temple, *i.e.*, he holds a little land on nominal terms from the temple property, in consideration for which he must fulfil certain requirements for the temple as on occasions of festivals. His office also invests him with certain rights in the community. The Vannân has, I believe, immense power indirectly, in the matter of giving or not giving new cloths to women after menstruation, but my information on the point is incomplete. Each receives from the temple daily during the festival a fixed quantity of rice, and their families are fed. Thus the tailor, the goldsmith, and the blacksmith, are under obligation to work as it may be required for the temple without remuneration in the ordinary way of labour, but for the honour only.

In the afternoon of the same day (the fifth) the Vannân and a Manûtan, the one following the other and not together, bring two umbrellas to the temple ; Vannân bringing one of cloth, the other one of cadjan. I am not sure whether the cloth umbrella has been in possession of the Vannân, but think it has. At all events, when he now brings it to the temple it is in thorough repair, a condition for which he is responsible. The cadjan umbrella is a new one. Following these two as they walk solemnly, each with his umbrella, is a large crowd. There are the usual processions of Bhagavati on the elephant, encircling the temple thrice in the morning, at noon and at night. Nothing more is done on this day.

Early on the sixth day the headman of the Mukkuvans (fisherman), who by virtue of his headship is called the 'Arayân,' together with the blacksmith and the goldsmith comes to the temple followed by an interested crowd, but accompanied by no orchestra of drums. To the Arayân is given half a sack of rice for himself and his followers, a silver umbrella belonging to the temple is handed over to him to be used when he comes to the temple again in the evening. To the blacksmith is given the temple sword. The goldsmith receives the silver umbrella from the Arayân, and excutes on it any repairs that may be needful ; and in like manner the blacksmith looks to the sword.

In the afternoon the headman of the Tîyans called the "Tandân," comes to the temple followed by two of his castemen carrying slung on a pole over their shoulders three bunches of young cocoanuts, an appropriate offering, the Tîyans being those whose ordinary profession is climbing the cocoanut palm, drawing the toddy, securing the cocoanuts, etc. This time there will be loud drumming and a large crowd with the Tandân, and in front of him are men dancing about, imitating sword play with sticks and shields, clanging the shields, pulling at bows as if firing off imaginary arrows, the while shouting and yelling *madly*. The sticks represent swords. Then come the blackmith and the goldsmith with the sword. The goldsmith has some responsibility connected with the sword, perhaps on account of its ornamentation, although the ordinary Malayali blacksmith is quite equal to the ordinary work of a goldsmith as well as repairing clocks and watches. Following comes the Arayân with the silver umbrella to an accompaniment of very noisy drumming; he and his umbrella in great state under a canopy of red cloth held lengthways by two men, one before, one behind. The procession of Bhagavati continues throughout the night, and ceases at day-break. These six days of the festival are called Vilakku.

A word about the drumming. The number of instrumentalists increases as the festival goes on, and on the last day I counted over fifty, all Nâyars. The instruments were the ordinary tom-tom, a skin stretched tight over one side of a circular wooden band, about 1½ feet in diameter and 2 or 3 inches in width, and the common long drum much narrower at the ends than in the middle, and there were (I think) a few of those narrow in the middle, something like an hour-glass cut short at both ends. They are beaten with drum-sticks, curved, not straight, thicker at the end held in the hand. The accuracy with which they were played on, never a wrong stroke, was truly amazing, although the rhythm was being changed perpetually; and their crescendo and diminuendo, from a perfect fury of wildness to the gentlest pianissimo, was equally astonishing, especially when we consider the fact that there was no visible leader of this strange orchestra.

Early on the seventh and last day, when the morning procession is over, there comes to the temple a man of the Pânan* caste. He carries a small cadjan umbrella which he has made himself, adorned all round the edges with a fringe of the young leaves of the cocoanut palm. His approach is heralded and noised just as in the case of the others on the previous day. The umbrella he brings should have a long handle and with this umbrella in his hand he performs a dance before the temple. The Malabar umbrella has a very long handle as a rule, in fact the correct way to carry an umbrella is with the end of the handle resting in the hand while the arm is straight at the side.

The temple which is figured in the plate is situated within a hollow square enclosure, which none in caste

---

* Pânan, a caste numerically small, and inferior. They make umbrellas of cadjan and perform at temples.

below the Nâyar is permitted to enter. To the north, south, east, and west, there is a level entrance into this hollow square, and beyond this entrance no man of inferior caste may go. The Pânan receives a certain quantity, about 10 lb. of raw rice for his performance.

In the afternoon a small crowd of Vettuvars come to the temple carrying with them swords, not very dangerous ones, and about ten small baskets made of cocoanut palm leaves, containing salt.* These baskets are carried slung on a pole as before. These men dance and shout in much excitement, cutting their heads with their own swords in their frenzy. Some of them represent devils or some kind of inferior evil spirits, and dance madly, under the influence of these spirits which they represent. Then comes the Arayân as on the previous day with his little procession, and lastly comes the blacksmith with the sword.

It is explained by the Malayalis that the individuals of the various castes who hold the office of tailor, goldsmith and so on to the temple, do so, not for the sake of what they receive from the temple, but in order to mark their position of superiority in their caste. The ceremonial allotted to each also no doubt marks his position in the ladder of caste.

The procession in the evening of this the seventh and last day is a great affair. Eight elephants which kept line beautifully, took part in this when I witnessed it. One of them very handsomely caparisoned had on its back a priest (Mûssad) carrying a sword smothered in garlands of red flowers representing the goddess. Up to this time, when she is represented by a sword, it will be remembered she has been represented by an image. The elephant bearing the priest with the sword is bedizened on the forehead with two golden discs, one on each side of the forehead, and over the centre of the forehead hangs a long golden ornament.† He bears other jewels, and over his back is a large canopy-like red cloth richly wrought. Before the elephant walked a Nâyar carrying in his right hand in front of him a sword of the kind

---

* The use of salt here is obscure as to the purpose. I remember a case of a Nâyar's house having been plundered, the idol was knocked down and salt was put in the place where it should have stood. The act was looked on as most insulting.

† The discs on the elephant's forehead are common in Malabar in affairs of ceremony. The Mappila poets are very fond of comparing a beautiful girl's breast to these cup-like discs.

called nândakam smeared with white (probably sandalwood) paste. The shape of this sword is given in the illustration. To its edge, at intervals of a few inches, are fastened tiny bells, so that, when it is shaken, there is a general jingle.

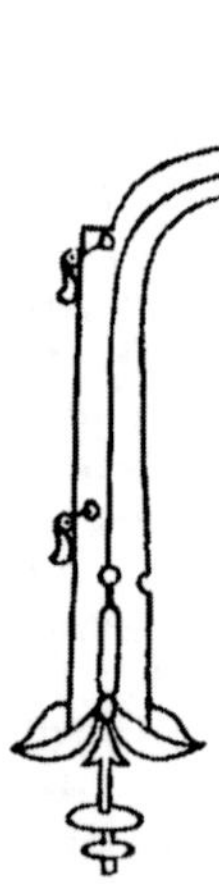

But just before the procession begins there is something for the Tîyans to do. Four men of this caste, having with them Pûkkalasams (flower-kalasams) and five having with them Jannakalasams (?) run along the west, north, and east, sides of the temple (outside the enclosure) shouting and making a noise more like the barking of dogs than anything else. The kalasams contain arrack which is presently given to the temple to be used in the ceremonies. Members of certain families only are allowed to perform in this business, and for what they do each man receives five edangâlis of rice from the temple and a small piece of the flesh of the goat to be sacrificed later. These nine men eat only once a day during the festival; they do no work, remaining quietly at home unless when at the temple; they cannot approach any one of caste lower than their own; they cannot cohabit with women; and they cannot see a women in menstruation during these days. A crowd of Tîyans join more or less in this, rushing about and barking like dogs, making a hideous noise. They too have kalasams, and, when they are tired of rushing and barking, they drink the arrack in them. These men are always under vow. In doing what they do, they fulfil their vow for the benefit they have already received from the goddess—cure from sickness as a rule. To the west of the temple is a circular pit—it was called the fire-pit, but there was no fire in it—and this pit all the Tîyan women of the neighbourhood circumambulate, passing from west round by north, three times, holding on the head a pewter plate on which are a little rice, bits of plantain leaves and cocoanut, and a burning wick. As each women completes her third round, she stands for a moment at the western side, facing east, and throws the contents of the plate into the pit, then goes to the western gate of the enclosure, and puts down her plate for an instant while she makes profound salaam to the goddess ere going away.

And now the procession starts out from the temple, issuing from the northern gate, and for a moment confronts a being so strange that he demands description. Of the many familiar demons of the Malayalis the two most intimate are "Kuttichchâttan" and "Gulikan," who are supposed to have assisted Kâli (who is scarcely the Kâli of Brâhmanism by the by) in overcoming the Asura, and on the occasion of this festival these two demons dance before her. "Gulikan" is represented by the Vannân and "Kuttichchâttan" by the Manûtan who have been mentioned already, and who are under like restrictions with the nine Tîyans. I saw poor "Gulikan" being made up, the operation occupying five or six hours or more before his appearance. I asked who he was and was told he was "a devil." He looked mild enough; but then his "make up" had just begun. He was lying flat on the ground close by the northern entrance of the enclosure, where presently he was to dance, a man painting his face to make it hideous and frightful. This done, his hair was dressed; large bangles were put on his arms, covering them almost completely from the shoulder to the wrist; his head and neck was swathed and decorated; a wooden platform arrangement from which hung a red ornamented skirt was fastened to his hips; there was fastened to his back an elongated Prince of Wales's feathers arrangement (made of plank) the top of which reached five feet above his head; and he was made to look like nothing human. Kuttichchâttan was treated in much the same manner.

As the procession issues from the northern gate of the temple where it is joined by the elephants, Gulikan stands in the northern entrance of the enclosure (which he cannot enter), facing it, and a halt is made for three minutes, while Gulikan dances. The poor old man who represented this fearful being, grotesquely terrible in his wonderful metamorphosis, must have been extremely glad when his three minutes' dance, preparation for which occupied all the afternoon, was concluded, for the mere weight and uncomfortable arrangement of his paraphernalia must have been extremely exhausting. It was with difficulty that he moved at all, let alone dance.

The procession passes round by east, where, at the entrance of the enclosure, Kuttichchâttan gives his dance, round by south to the westward, and leaving the enclosure proceeds to a certain banyan tree under which is a high raised platform built up with earth and stones. Preceding the procession at a distance of 50 yards are the nine men of the Tîyan caste, mentioned already, carrying kalasams on their heads, and a crowd of women of the same caste, each one carrying a pewter plate—*larger* than the plates used when encircling the fire pit—on which are rice, etc., and the burning wick as before. The plate and its contents on this occasion as well as before is called talapôli. I could not make out that anything in particular is done at the banyan tree, and the procession soon returns to the temple, the nine men and the Tîyan women following, carrying their kalasams and talapôli. On the way, a number of cocks are given in sacrifice by people under a vow. In the procession are a number of "devil dancers" garlanded with white flowers of the pagoda tree mixed with red, jumping, gesticulating, shouting, in an avenue of the crowd in front of the elephant bearing the sword. The person under a vow holds the cock towards one of these "devil dancers" who (never ceasing his gyrations, mad-like gestures and contortions), presently seizes its head, wrings it off, and flings it high in the air. The vows which are fulfilled by this rude decapitation of cocks have been made in order to bring about cure for some ailment.

The procession passes through the temple yard, the enclosure, from west to east, and proceeds half a mile to a banyan tree under which, like the other, there is a high raised platform. When passing by the temple, the Tîyan women empty the contents of their plates in the fire pit as before, and the nine men hand over the arrack in their kalasams to the temple servants. Let us note here as we go along the curious distribution of this rice which is heaped in the fire pit. Two-thirds of it go to the four Tîyans carrying the Pû (flower) kalasams and one-third to the five who carried the Jannakalasams. Returning to the procession, we find it at the raised platform to the east of the temple. On this platform have been placed already an ordinary bamboo quart-like measure of paddy, and one of rice, each covered with a plantain leaf. The principal devil dancer takes a handful of rice and paddy and flings it all around. The procession then visits in turn the gates of the gardens of the four owners of the temple. At each is the measure of rice and the measure of paddy covered with plaintain leaves as before, beside them

PL. XIV.

A NAYAR HOME, PANUR, N. MALABAR. THE BATHING TANK AND BATHING SHED IN THE FOREGROUND.

a small lamp or burning wick, and the devil dancer throws a handful towards the house. It then finds its way to the tree to the west under which, on the platform, is now a measure of paddy and a lamp; some Brâhmans* repeat mantrams and the elephant, the priest on his back and the sword in his hand, all three, are supposed to tremble violently. Up to this time the procession has moved leisurely, a very slow march. Now, starting suddenly, it proceeds at a run to the temple where the priest descends quickly from the elephant and is taken inside the temple by the Mûssad priests. He who has been carrying the sword all this time places it on the sill of the door of the room in which it is kept for worship, and prostrates before it. The sword then shakes itself for 15 minutes! until the chief priest stays its agitation by sprinkling on it some tirtam, fluid made sacred by having been used for anointing the image of the goddess. This done, the chief amongst the devil dancers will with much internal tumult as well as outward convolutions say, in the way of oracle, whether the Dêvi has been pleased with the festival in her honour, or not. As he pronounces this oracular utterance he falls in a sort of swoon, and every soul, excepting only the priests and the temple servants, leaves the place as quickly as possible. The sheds which have been erected for temporary habitation around the temple will be quickly demolished, and search will be made round about to make sure that no one remains near while the mystic rite of sacrifice is about to be done. When the whole place has been cleared, the four owners of the temple, the senior members of the Taravâds who stand in the position of owners and who, by the way, have stayed, hand over each a goat with a rope tied round its neck to the chief priest; and as soon as they have done so they too depart. There will remain now in the temple three Mûssads, one drummer (Marayar) and two temple servants: no others. These Mûssads are commonly called Brâhmans though the Nambûtiris do not admit them to be such. The reason for all this secrecy seems to lie in objection to let it be known generally that any sacrifice is done. I was told again and again that there was no such thing. It is a mystic secret. The Mûssad priests repeat mantrams over the goats for an hour as a preliminary to the sacrifice. Then

* East Coast Brahmans (Pattar) I think: perhaps Mûssads.

the chief priest dons a red silk cloth and takes in his hand a chopper-like sword in shape something like a a small bill-hook—while the goats are taken to a certain room within the temple. This room is rather a passage than a room as there are to it but two walls, running north and south. The goats are made to stand in turn in the middle of this room, facing to the south ; the chief priest stand to the east of a goat facing west as he cuts off its head with the chopper. He never ceases his mantrams and the goats never flinch,—the effect of the mantrams! Several cocks are then sacrified in the same place, and over the carcasses of goats and cocks there is sprinkled charcoal powder mixed in water (karutta gurusi) and saffron powder and lime water (chukanna gurusi), the flow of mantrams never ceasing the while. The three Mûssads only see the sacrifice, a part of the rite supremely secret. Equally so is that which follows. The carcass of one goat will be taken out of the temple by the northern door to the north side of the temple; and from this place one of the temple servants, *who is blindfolded*, drags it three times round the temple, the Mûssads following closely repeating their mantrams, the drummer in front beating his drum softly with his fingers. The drummer dare not look behind him and does not know what is being done. After the third round the drummer and the temple servant go away and the three Mûssads cook some of the flesh of the goats and one or two of the cocks (or a part of one) with rice. This rice when cooked is taken to the kâvu (grove), to the north of the temple, and there the Mûssads again ply their mantrams. As each mantram is ended a handful of saffron powder is flung on the rice, and all the time the drummer who by this time has returned, the only one present with the priests, keeps up an *obligato pianissimo* with his drum, using his fingers : he faces the north and the priests face the south. Presently, having done with the mantrams, the priests run (*not walk*) once round the temple carrying the cooked rice and scattering it wide as they go, repeating their mantrams. They enter the temple and remain within until day-break. No one can leave the temple until morning comes. Before daybreak the temple is thoroughly swept and cleaned, and then the Mûssads go out and the five Nambûtiris again enter before sunrise and perform the ordinary worship thrice in the day. For this one day only. The next morning the Mûssad priests return and resume their duties.

Men and women who have taken part in the festival are considered to have undergone spiritual purification each in his or her own caste, and to have marked their position in it as well as in the social scale.

Beyond noting that the weirdness of the human tumult busy in its religious effusion is on the last night enhanced by fireworks, mere description of the scene of the festival will not be attempted, and such charming adjuncts of it as the gallery of pretty Nâyar women looking on from the garden fence at the seething procession in the lane below must be left to the imagination for the present, while we must be content with such accuracy as we may attain on all points: neither fancy nor beauty shall allure us from the dull path of precision, for the mere features of the ceremonial are one real concern.

It will have been noticed that the Nambûtiris hold aloof from the festival: they purify the temple before and after, but no more.

The importance attached to the various offices of those who are attached to the temple by however slender a thread, was illustrated by a rather amusing squabble between two of the Mukkuvans (fishermen), an uncle and nephew, as to which of them should receive the silver umbrella from the temple and bear it to the house of the goldsmith to be repaired. How the squabble arose, how indeed there could have arisen a squabble on such a point as seniority between an uncle and a nephew amongst Mukkuvans, whose descent is reckoned from father to son, I know not, but during the festival one of them made a rapid journey to the Zamorin (about 50 miles distant), paid some fees and established himself as the senior who had the right to carry the umbrella. There are points of resemblance between this festival and the village festival of Southern India where the buffalo "devoted" to the goddess of the village is sacrificed, where there is the slaughter of the lamb by the strong teeth of a man, the dressing up in leaves, the man naked and blindfolded going round outside the village while cooked rice and blood are scattered wide, the blindfolded man falling senseless before the goddess at the end of it.*

There are many festivals in Malabar description of which would be very interesting, but information in detail is wanting in my notes, so I must perforce rest content with what has been related of the festival at the

* Described at length by me in the "Journal of the Anthropological Society of Bombay" some eight years ago.

Pishâri Kâvu which represents one of moderate importance and truly one of the people, and its narration is fairly complete. It seems to express the religion of the Nâyars as it is when not tacked on to that of the Brâhmans: as they formulate it of themselves entirely in their own way.

An important local festival is that held near Palghat, in November, in the little suburb Kalpâti inhabited entirely by Pattar Brâhmans from the east; but it is not a true Malayali festival and it suffices to mention its existence for it in no way represents the religion of the Nâyar. The dragging of cars on which are placed the images of deities, common everywhere from the temple of Jagganath, at Pûri in Orrisa, to Cape Comorin, is quite unknown in Malabar excepting only at Kalpâti which is close to the eastern frontier of Malabar. The Kalpâti festival is the only "car festival" in Malabar.

Near Chowghât (Chavagât), about 30 miles to the southward of Calicut, on the backwater, an arm of the sea and separated from it by a thin strip of land between the rivers, at a place called Guruvayûr, is a very important temple the property of the Zamorin, yielding a very handsome revenue. I visited this festival on one occasion and saw there much which was of interest but which must find place in the account of regions of others than Nâyars. Here purchase was made of a few offerings such as are made to the temple in satisfaction of vows. A very rude representation of an infant in silver, a hand, a leg, an ulcer, a pair of eyes, and, most curious of all, a silver string which represents a man—the giver. Symbolization of the offering of self is made by a silver string as long as the giver is tall! Goldsmiths working in silver and gold are to be seen just outside the gate of the temple ready to provide at a moment's notice the object any person intends to offer, in case he is not already in possession of his votive offering.

The subject of vows can be touched on but incidentally here.* A vow is made by one desiring offspring, to have his hand or leg cured, to have an ulcer cured, to fulfil any desire whatsoever, and he decides in solemn affirmation to himself (it is not necessary to go to a temple for the purpose of vowing) to give a silver image of a child, a silver

* The subject of vows generally, including description of a Roman Catholic shrine at Cochin somewhat akin to that at Guravayûr, was treated by me in an article which appeared in the 'Calcutta Review' for January 1899.

leg, and so on, in the event of his having fulfilment of his desire. The offering is never an adjunct of the prayers; it is always something done for benefit received. The thing to be noted is that a vow is *always* fulfilled; fulfilled as well as the vower can possibly fulfil it; it is never forgotten or overlooked.

> "When the devil was sick the devil a saint would be
> "When the devil was well the devil a saint was he"

is a couplet inapplicable to the Nâyar, or, indeed, to any people in Southern India, where vows, of objects to be given or animals to be sacrified, are treated always with the utmost sacredness even by people who perhaps in no relation of life behave for an hour with common honesty.

A true Malayali festival is that held at Kottiôr, in North Malabar, in the forest at the foot of the Wynâd hills rising 3,000 to 5,000 feet from the sides of the little glade where it is situated. It is held in July during the height of the monsoon rain. The average rainfall at Kottiôr in July is probably 60 inches at least, so the devotees generally get a good ducking. Though it is a festival for high and low these do not mix at Kottiôr. The Nâyars go first, and after a few days, the Nâyars having done, the Tîyans, and so on. A curious feature of it is that people going to attend it are distinctly rowdy, feeling they have a right to abuse in the vilest and filthiest terms everyone they see on the way—perhaps a few days' march; and not only do they abuse to their hearts' content in their exhuberant excitement, but they use personal violence to person and property all along the road. They return like lambs.

I have not been able to ascertain with that definiteness which would enable me to offer more than an opinion, the connection between this violence of language and physical force against innocent people who are met *en route*, and the object of worship at Kottiôr, so will leave that part of the subject alone. The other day I visited the Gangamma festival at sacred Tirupati in North Arcot, and observed, together with conduct the most truly religious vows being carried out with the strongest disregard to personal comfort, the use of language truly filthy and obscene *towards the goddess herself!* "Gangamma! You have a—— (using a filthy word for the vagina) as big as a basket." "She is a whore" said another; and each one in the little crowd of votaries, evidently from the same village, as they approached the shrine, tried to out-do the other in insult and vituperation of the goddess to whom they had come to pay their vows for some good done them by her. Obscenities which need not be described were done—these chiefly by people of very low caste let it be said—by people who felt that neither gesture in the dance nor word could be gross enough to express the violence of their feelings. Yet these people, men and women, rolled, or were rolled, for they soon become unconscious, many times round the temple, their arms stretched towards it, their hair, their clothes (scanty enough) and persons generally thick with the dust. A piteous sight. And there were to be seen men carrying over their heads an ornamented wooden canopy, the whole (and no light weight) held up, fastened to the person by the ends of the supports of the canopy, being stuck through the skin of the back and of the chest. Nothing resting on the shoulders or held in the hand. I saw a man who, to fulfil a vow to this goddess who was abused so vilely, had done this every year for over twenty years, and this year handed on performance of the painful vow to his son, a growing lad. The bearers of these canopies danced continuously as if trying to make the points in their flesh as hurtful as possible. So that, together with vituperation of the goddess, there was much veneration, and there is no hesitation in expressing this through bodily discomfort and pain.

Content for the present with this example from another part of the Presidency, we will return now to Kottiôr which I visited in November 1894. One sees a temple of Isvara, there called Perumâl (or Perumâl Iswara) by the people; a low thatched building forming a hollow square, in the centre of which was the shrine which, I was not permitted to see. There were some Nambûtiri priests who came out and entered into conversation. Their life far away in the forest must be a lonely one. The refreshment which they offered, butter-milk and sugar, was accepted thankfully. The Nambûtiris, very unsophisticated persons and much wrapped up in their personal sanctity, placed the milk and sugar on the ground, and invited us graciously to partake. A large piece of cocoanut which they threw to my dog was, strange to say, eaten greedily by the beast.

The festival is not held at the temple but in the forest about quarter of a mile distant. This spot is deemed extremely sacred and dreadful. There was, however, no objection to myself and my companion visiting it: we were simply begged not to go. There were with us a

Nâyar and a Kurichchan, and the faces of these men when we proceeded to wade through the little river, knee-deep and about 30 yards wide, in order to reach the sacred spot of the festival, expressed anxious wonder. They dared not accompany us across. No one (excepting, of course, a Muhammadan) would go near the place unless during the few days of the festival when it is safe: at all other times any man going to the place is destroyed instantly. How much this belief has to do with Îswara need not be commented on! Nothing on earth would have persuaded either the Nâyar or the Kurichchin to cross that river. Orpheus proceeding to find his Eurydice, Dante about to enter the Inferno had not embarked on so fearful a journey! About a hundred yards beyond the stream we came upon the sacred spot, a little glade in the forest. Why this uncomfortable place was chosen I know not; in the rains when the festival is held it is usually under water, and the people have to stand in water. In the centre of the glade is a circle of piled up stones, 12 feet in diameter. In the middle of the pile of stones is a rude lingam. By the same token the lingam had been broken and displaced a few days previously by some Mâppilas searching for treasure which they thought was there. *Running east from the circle of the lingam is a long shed, in the middle of which is a long raised platform of brick, used apparently as a place for cooking. Around the lingam there were also thatched sheds in which the people had lodged during the festival. Grass and weeds were growing high, and the sheds were dilapidated and looking as if they had not been used for years; but then the rain in Malabar brings about destructive effects with astonishing rapidity.

Pilgrims going to this festival carry with them offerings of some kind. Tîyans take young cocoanuts. I am not

---

* The circle of stones is specially interesting. Near the Angadipuram-Manjery road, between Vellila and the ferry is a monolith in the centre of a piled up platform circled with stones, the circle 30 feet in diameter. Apparently one of the many pre-Hindu remains in Malabar. Description of the ancient remains in Malabar, which are specially interesting, must be made later on. Just now let me note that stone circles are common. And I find in my notes the following: "On the hill side just about the Tirunelli temple (North Wynâd forests), where there is a clearing in the forest and the ground is somewhat flat, is a circle of stones 12 feet in diameter, and filled up with earth so as to make a raised platform nearly 2 feet in height; in the centre a small upright stone 10 inches high. To the north-east, three flat upright stones . . . . and a flat place, rudely square about 11 feet from the circle, evidently an old sacred place of some of the jungle folk."

sure what the Nâyars take; perhaps the same. Every one who returns brings with him a swish made of split young leaves of the cocoanut palm.

A shrine to which the Malayalis, Nâyars included, resort is that of Subramania in Palni, in the north-west corner of the Madura district, about a week's march from the confines of Malabar near Palghat. Not only are vows paid to this shrine, but men, letting their hair grow for a year after their father's death, proceed to have it cut there. The plate shows an ordinary Palni pilgrim. The arrangement which he is carrying is called a kâvadi. There are two kinds of kâvadi: a milk kâvadi (one containing milk in a pot) and a fish kâvadi (one containing fish). The vow may be made in respect of either, each being appropriate to certain circumstances. When the time comes near for the pilgrim to start for Palni he dresses in reddish orange cloths, shoulders his kâvadi and starts out. Together with a man ringing a bell, and perhaps one with a tom-tom, with ashes on his face, he assumes the role of beggar. The well-to-do are inclined to reduce the beggar period to the minimum; but a beggar every votary must be, and as a beggar he goes to Palni in all humbleness and humiliation, and there he fulfils his vow; leaves his kâvadi and his hair and a small sum of money.

Though the individuals about to be noticed were not Nâyars, their cases illustrate very well the religious idea of the Nâyar as expressed under certain circumstances; for between the Nâyars and these there is in this respect little if any differenee. It was at Guruvayûr in November 1895. On a high raised platform under a peepul tree were a number of people under vows, bound for Palni. A boy of 14 had suffered as a child from epilepsy, and seven years ago his father vowed for him (on his behalf) that if he were cured he would make the pilgrimage to Palni. He wore a string of beads round his neck and a like string on his right arm (these were in some way connected with the vow). His head was bent and he sat motionless under his kâvadi, leaning on the bar, which when he carried it rested on his shoulder. He could not go to Palni until it was revealed to him in a dream when he was to start. He had waited for this dream seven years, subsisting on roots (yams, etc.) and milk,—no rice. Now he had had the long-looked-for dream, and he was about to start. As an instance of the Malayali's ignorance of the Hindu theogony, this youth said he was going to the god "Sri Krishnan" in Palni. It is well known that god there is *not* Krishna.

Another pilgrim was a man wearing an oval band of silver over the lower portion of the forehead almost covering his eyes; his tongue outside his teeth, kept in position by a silver skewer through it. Had been fasting two years. Much under the influence of the god, and whacking incessantly at a drum in delirious excitement. The skewer was put in the day before, and was to be left in for forty days. Several of the pilgrims wore a handkerchief tied over the mouth, they being under a vow of silence. One poor man wore the regular instrument of silence, the mouth-lock (a wide silver band over the mouth, the ends reaching over the cheeks, a skewer through both cheeks keeping the ends together * and, of course, the mouth open); and he sat patiently in a nice tent-like affair, about 3 feet high. People fed him with milk, &c., but he made no effort to procure food, relying merely on what was given him.

Pilgrims generally go in crowds under charge of a priestly guide, one who, having made a certain number of journeys to the shrine, wears a peculiar sash and other gear. They call themselves pujâris, and are quite *au fait* with all the ceremonial prior to the journey as well as with the exigencies of the road. As I stood there, one of these pujâris stood up amidst the recumbent crowd. He raised his hands towards the temple a little to the west, then spread out his hands as if invoking a blessing on the people around him. Full of religious fervour he was (apparently at any rate) unconscious of all but the spiritual need of his flock.

The use of the mouth-lock is common with the Nâyars when they assume the pilgrims' robes and set out for Palni, and I have often seen many of them garbed and mouth-locked going off on a pilgrimage to that place.

Brief mention must be made of the festival held at Kodungallûr in the northernmost corner of the Cochin State, along the coast, as it possesses some strange features peculiar to Malabar and is much frequented by the Nâyars. Kodungallûr is near Cranganore, the old Dutch Settlement, where was, probably, the Musiris of the Greeks. Tiruvangaikalam, close by, will probably turn out to be the long lost site of the capital of the Chêra kingdom. I have been disappointed in obtaining particulars

* The mouth-lock is not peculiar to Malabar. A description of this form of vow in another part of the Presidency was made by me in the "Journal of the Anthropological Society of Bombay," Vol. II, No. 2 (1890).

of the festival, so make the following excerpt from Mr. Logan's well-known "Manual of Malabar." "It takes the people in great crowds from their homes. The whole country near the lines of march rings with the shouts 'Nada-a Nada-a' of the pilgrims to the favourite shrines, chief of which is that at Cranganore (Kodungallûr) in the Native State of Cochin. Of what takes place when the pilgrims reach this spot perhaps the less said the better. In their passage up to the shrine the cry of 'Nada-a Nada-a' (march, march away) is varied by terms of unmeasured abuse levelled at the goddess (a Bhagavati) of the shrine. This abusive language is supposed to be acceptable to her. On arrival at the shrine they desecrate it in every conceivable way, believing that this too is acceptable; they throw stones and filth, howling volleys of opprobrium at her house. The chief of the fisherman caste, styled *Kûli Muttatta Arayan*, has the privilege of being the first to begin the work of polluting the *Bhoot* or shrine. Into other particulars it is unnecessary to enter; cocks are slaughtered and sacrificed. The worshipper gets flowers only, and no holy water after paying his vows. Instead of water he proceeds outside and drinks arrack or toddy, which an attendant Nâyar serves out. All castes are free to go, including Tîyars and low caste people. The temple was originally only a Bhoot or holy tree with a platform. The image in the temple is said to have been introduced only of recent years." It is a pity Mr. Logan is so reticent. My information is that the headman of the Mukkuvans (fisher caste) opens the festival by solemnly making a fœcal deposit on the image. Here again there is the same strange union of everything that is filthy, abusive, foul and irreverent, with every mode of expressing the deepest religious feeling.

Leaving now the religion, expression of which may be seen at temple festivals and during pilgrimages to these scenes of religious fervour, we will turn to that which we see in the house of the Nâyar at home.

Plate XII shows a man standing with a sword of the shape known as Nândakam. He is an individual called a Velichchappâd, and as he stood to be photographed by me his forehead and face streamed with blood from a self-inflicted wound on the head. The Velichchappâd is a familiar character in Malabar. His profession illustrates the very mixed character of the Hinduism of the Nâyar, partaking as it does of much of the lower cult,—animism,

PL. XV.

AYYAPPAN TEMPLE, NEAR CALICUT.

and deification of ancestors, worship of snakes and kites, ceremonies connected therewith, sacrifice, magic, witchcraft and sorcery—together with the purest form of Vêdic Brâhmanism known in Southern India, of which there is the highest expression in the temples attached to the wealthy Nambûtiri Illams, to which the Nâyar goes daily to pray, to purify his mind after having purified his body by bathing. There is very little to be seen of prayer in Southern India outside Malabar. The great mass of the people (I exclude the Brâhmans, a very minute percentage of the whole) never dream of going to a temple daily to pray; in fact prayer for its own sake scarcely exists. People go in crowds to a temple on the occasion of a festival to make obeisance to the god, and in a vague way to pray, or they will go to fulfil a vow; but going merely to pray by way of self purification of spirit is certainly rare, for this denotes a phase of religion to which the great mass of the people of Southern India has not reached.

Far away in, as it may be said, rural Malabar, I witnessed the ceremony in which the Velichchappâd exhibited his quality. It was in the courtyard of a Nâyar house, to which thronged all the neighbours (Nâyars), men and pretty women, boys and girls. The ceremony lasts about an hour. The Nâyar said it was the custom in his family to have it done once a year, but could give no account of how the custom had originated: most probably in a vow; some ancestor having vowed that if such or such benefit be received, he will for ever after have an annual performance of this ceremony in his house. It involved some expenditure, as the Velichchappâd had to be paid, and the neighbours had to be fed. Somewhere about the middle of the little courtyard, always as clean as a dinner table, the Velichchappâd placed a lamp (of the Malabar pattern) having a lighted wick, a kalasam, which he had prepared, some flowers, camphor, saffron and other paraphernalia. Bhagavati was the deity invoked, and the business involved offering flowers, and waving a lighted wick around the kalasam. The Velichchappâd's movements became quicker, and suddenly seizing the sword he ran round the courtyard (*against* the sun, as the sailors say) shouting wildly. He is under the influence of the deity who has been induced into him, and he gives oracular utterance to the deity's commands. What he said I know not, and no one else seemed to know or care in the least, much interested though they were in the performance. As he ran, every now and then he cut his forehead with the strange misshapen sword, pressing it against the skin and sawing (vertically) up and down. The blood streamed all over his face. Presently he became wilder and wilder, and whizzed round the lamp, bending forward towards the kalasam. Evidently some deity, some spirit, was present here, and spoke through the mouth of the Velichchappâd. This, I think, undoubtedly represents the belief of all who were present. When he had done whizzing round the kalasam, he soon became a normal being and stood before my camera. The fee for this self-inflicted laceration is one rupee and some odds and ends of rice, etc. I saw the Velichchappâd about three days afterwards going to perform elsewhere. The wound on his forehead had healed! The careful observer can always identify a Velichchappâd by the triangular-like patch over the forehead where the hair will not grow, and where the skin is somewhat indurated. The Velichchappâds seem to get used to cutting their foreheads as the eels to skinning.

We shall find the oracle again when we come to the lower races. I have seen a fine demonstration of it amongst the Paniyans of Wynâd when engaged in a regular corrobboree. An extremely interesting example of this combination of this phase of the lower Dravidian cult which is in no way Hindu, with the Brâhmanic religion, is to be seen at Mailâr in the Bellary district. There the oracle is bound up with a story about Rishis and Asuras, an incarnation of Siva and Pârvati, and many thousands assemble yearly to hear the oracle delivered by a man on the top of a huge affair representing Siva's bow, speaking the words of the god.

Before concluding the subject of religion, allusion must be made to the worship of ancestors. Cremation of the dead, as in the case of the Nambûtiris, is done in the garden or compound surrounding the Taravâd house, in the south or south-west corner of it; so the Nâyar has the ashes and spirits of his ancestors with him always. We have seen already how that pacification of the spirits of those who have passed from view, and who are in the land of the shades, pervade the lives of the living. They are worshipped every new moon day, but especially on the new moon of Karkitakam,* of Tulâm and of Kumbham

---

* The names of the Malayali months have been given already—see Nambûtiris (Bulletin, Vol. III, No. 2).

months. The last is the day following Siva râtri, the well-known Hindu festival. As it was told to me "Food is offered to the ghosts" on these occasions; to all ancestors, male and female. Food of any kind except cooked rice is offered.* It is cooked and placed in the middle room on the west side of the house, where are kept small images in gold or silver of the senior members of the Taravâd (in poorer houses, a stone simply is put to represent the deceased), and the door will be shut for about ten minutes, after which the food will be removed and eaten by the house people. Special worship of ancestors is often made at the temples specially sacred, on the new moons which have been specified, especially on the last. The plate depicts the crowd in the bed of the Ponnâni river on the day following Siva râtri. Men and women bathed and put on clean cloths and, when they had done so put a little burning camphor, sandalwood powder and some other little accessories, on a leaf which was floated down the river after a brief prayer. The scene of the picture adjoins the temple at Tirunavâyi, supposed to be the oldest in Malabar.

SERPENT WORSHIP.

Description, such as is here attempted, of the Nâyar's religion is incomplete so far. There remains to say something of serpent worship and to make some allusion to common superstitions. For description of these I would refer the interested reader to a capital little book entitled "Malabar and its Folk" published by Messrs. Natesan & Co., Madras, by Mr. T. K. Gopal Panniker, B.A., himself a Nâyar as his name denotes. With this gentleman's permission I will reproduce here chapter 12 of his book entitled "Serpent Worship in Malabar":—

" Malabar is a country which preserves to this day primitive institutions of a type peculiarly fascinating to the ethnologist. Of the various kinds of primitive worship still practised in the country that of the serpent occupies a prominent place. Here the serpent is deified and offerings of pooja are often made to the reptile. It has got a powerful hold upon the popular imagination. Each household has got its own serpent deity possessing large powers for good as well as for evil. A separate spot is set apart in the house-compound as the abode of these deities. This reserved spot is converted into a small jungle almost circular in

* Bread made of rice flour may be offered.

shape. It is overgrown with trees of various kinds, and shrubs, and sometimes medicinal plants also. In the middle of this quasi-circular shrine images usually made of laterite after specified shapes are arranged in certain established methods and a passage is opened to the seat of these images from outside. This spot is so scrupulously reserved, that not even domestic animals are allowed to stray therein. No trees from the place are to be felled down, nor any plant whatever for that matter with any metal or more particularly iron weapons; for these are unholy things, the introduction alone of which inside the sanctified area, not to say the actual cutting down of the tree, is regarded as exceedingly distasteful to these serpent gods. They are not to be desecrated by the touch or even by the approach of a low-caste man. Once in every year at least poojah offerings are made to these gods through the medium of the Numbûdri priests.

" Periodical ceremonies called Pāmbantullel are performed to propitiate them. These are resorted to only on special occasions for the purpose of averting serious visitations from the family. The ceremony is a long complicated process. Any individual drawn from among the Nairs themselves is capable of acting the part of priests on these occasions. A day is fixed for the opening of the ceremony; and a particular plot of ground in the house yard is cleansed and preserved for the performance of the poojahs incidental to the ceremony. Then on the spot certain square figures are drawn, one inside another, and these are tastefully diversified by the interpolation of circular figures and others inside and about them, based on geometrical principles. A peculiar symmetry is observed in the matter of these figures. The figures used in the drawings are usually of various colours, red, white, black and others. Ordinary rice-flour, then again such flour mixed with a combination of chunnam and turmeric powder, thereby making the flour pure red, and burnt paddy husk are chiefly employed. Then a number of other accessories are also required for the ceremony in the shape of lamps, cocoanuts, eatables of various sorts prepared from paddy and rice and some other cooked things, such as rice, bread made of rice, and others. These are properly arranged in the place and poojah is offered by the priest with the slow recitation of *mantrams*, and some holy songs or ballads in memory of these gods. Then a number of Nair women, with perfect purity and cleanliness of person are seated close to each other in a row or two. These women are to preserve sanctity and purity of their persons by a total abstinence from animal food, intoxicants and anything else of an exciting nature for a prescribed period of time; and it is only after the lapse of this period that they become worthy of being admitted to this ceremony. Thus having purged their bodies of all worldliness they are taken into the ceremony and are seated as described before. Now by means of the *mantrams* and poojah the serpent gods are propitiated and in consequence they manifest themselves in the bodies of these female representatives of theirs. The entrance of the gods into their bodies is characterised by a fearful concussion of their whole frame, gradually developing into a ceaseless, shaking, particularly the upper parts. A few minutes afterwards, they begin to speak one by one and their speeches are regarded as expressions of the god's will. Sometimes the gods appear in the bodies of all these females and sometimes only in those of a select few or none at all. The refusal of the gods to enter into such persons is symbolical of some want of cleanliness and purity in them; which contingency is looked upon as a source of anxiety to the individual. It may also suggest the displeasure of these gods towards the family in respect of which the ceremony is performed. In either case, such refusal on the part of the gods is an index of their ill-will or dissatisfaction. In cases where the gods refuse to appear in any one of those seated for the purpose, the ceremony is prolonged until the gods are so properly propitiated as to constrain them to manifest themselves. Then after the lapse of the number of days fixed for the ceremony and after the will of the serpent gods is duly expressed the ceremonies close.

"One other small item of offering to these gods consists in certain ballads sung by the Pulluvar females going about from house to house at stated seasons of the year. They take a pretty large pitcher, close its opening by means of a small circular piece of thin leather which is fastened on to the vessel by means of strings strongly tied round its neck. Another string is adjusted to the leather cover which when played on by means of the fingers, produces a hoarse note which is said to please the god's ears, pacify their anger and lull them into sleep. This vessel is carried from house to house in the day time by these Pulluvar females; and placing the vessel in a particular position on the ground, and sitting in a particular fashion in relation to the vessel, they play on the string which then produces a very pleasing musical note. Then they sing ballads to the accompaniment of these notes. After continuing this for sometime they stop, and getting their customary dues from the family, go their own way. It is believed that these notes and the ballads are peculiarly pleasing to the serpent gods, who bless those for whose sakes the music has been rendered. In consequence of the halo of sanctity that has been popularly thrown round the serpent it is considered a sin of a most heinous nature to kill one of these deified reptiles. The killing of a cobra is regarded with the utmost concern amongst us. In such case the carcase is taken and duly burned with all the necessary solemn ceremonials. Sandalwood is the fuel used sometimes. A small pit is dug which is covered with sandalwood pieces and they are set fire to. When the flame burns intensely the body is quietly placed in it, and reduced to ashes together with, in some cases, incense and myrrh. This is believed to mitigate the dangers consequent on the death of the serpent.

"The popular conception of the family cobra is that it is a tiny little thing with a full developed hood, and fangs, and possessing a golden tinge; which shine brilliantly in the rays of the sun. At the sight of human beings it gets away to its holy shrine exhibiting a reeling motion on its way thither. It never gets far away from its abode of which it is the perennial guardian.

"One striking phase of serpent worship in Malabar relates to the family of Pappanmakkat Nambudris and the singular and effective control they exercise over serpents in general. Their powers are handed from father to son. It is said that this Nambudri household is full of cobras which find their abode in every nook and corner of it. The inmates can scarcely move about without placing their feet upon any one of these serpents. Owing to the magic influence of the family the serpents cannot and will not injure them. The serpents are said to be always at the beck and call of the members of this Nambudri family and render unquestioned obedience to their commands. They watch and protect the interests of the family in the most jealous spirit. In short, these reptiles live, move, and have their being as freely as if they were domesticated animals imbued with supernatural powers.

"Cases of cobra-poison are generally taken to this Brahman family and the headman sometimes summons before him the identical animal which caused injury and it is said successfully effects a cure as if by some mystic and magic influence.

"The serpent also plays a conspicuous part in contracts between citizens. The family serpent is in old deeds the subject-matter of sale. The sale of a house compound extends also to the family serpent. The stipulation in these documents invariably is that the family serpents are sold along with the properties; and even in cases of division of family property amongst its several branches of members, the family-serpent is included in the division. Such is the sacred prominence which has been given to the serpent amongst us. Their anger is said to manifest itself in some member of the family being struck down with leprosy or some other loathsome disease; while by their propitiation they can be converted into the guardian angels of our households, powerful enough to preserve the prosperity of the inmates as well as to vouchsafe their complete immunity from the attacks of virulent diseases and sometimes even from death."

As the subject of serpent-worship is one of fascinating interest, I will add to the preceding extract, which is as interesting as it is accurate, an excerpt from the "Report of the Census of Travancore" for 1891 (the Malayalam year 1066), a book which is perhaps not accessible to many. The shrine which is described therein is in the neighbouring Native State of Travancore, but it is equally representative of one in Malabar :—

"A serpent-kavoo in Travancore. Many places of Hindu worship exist in Travancore under groves locally known as kavoos. There are thousands of these in the country. Lieutenants Ward and Conner estimated their number at 15,000 seventy years ago. This number has, I think, increased since then. These kavoos are all dedicated to minor divinities such as Nàgathans, Nàgarajas, Yekshis, Gandharvas, and Sàstas. Some are of great age and repute and own enormous properties for their maintenance. One of these a well-known sarpa-kavoo in a village 70 miles north of Travancore will be here described. Mythological origin for these sarpa-kavoos is thus stated in the Kéralòlpatti. When Parasuràma's first colonists found Kérala uninhabitable and unimprovable, they abandoned it and returned to their old country. During the time of their absence the Nàgas (serpents) of the lower world, called in popular language Nàgalòkam or Pàtàla, took possession of the newly-reclaimed land and settled there. The colonists returning found that the serpents had usurped their lands, upon which a fight ensued, and Parasuràma arbitrated between his colonists and the Nàgas, wih the result that these latter were to be given a corner of every occupied compound. Thus arose the sarpa kavoos of Malabar which, as I have already described in a previous chapter, is generally at the south-west corner of every Tarvâd garden. And Parasuràma further ordained that the places allotted to the Nàgas were to be left untouched by the knife or the spade, thus enabling the underwood trees and creepers to grow luxuriantly therein. It is to such places that the name of kavoo (or grove) is given. In the kavoo are generally planted several idols of serpents on a stone basement called chittrakoodam, and sometimes a low wall is thrown round to prevent cattle or children trespassing into that space. The propitiation of the serpents is deemed essential for the well-being and prosperity of the householder. Offerings of noorum palum (dough and milk) of cooked rice, lights and songs are made periodically to the serpent gods in the kavoos. The one I am describing here is one of the most important in Travancore. This is known as Mannārsāla. Once upon a time, so says tradition, a male member of this Illam married a girl of the Vettikkòttu Illam, where the serpents were held in great veneration. The girl's parents being poor could give her nothing in the way of dowry. They, therefore, gave her one of the stone idols of the serpent, of which there were many in their house. This stone idol the girl was counselled to take care of and regularly worship; subsequently it is said the girl became a mother and brought forth a boy and a snake, whereupon the snake-child was located in the underground cellar of the house and brought up. The Illam prospered from that day. The woman and the snake are believed to be the cause of the affluence of the family, and to this day to the surname of the male members of that Illom are added, by way of distinction, the names of the serpent god and that of the female. Thus my informant, the present head of the family, is called Vasaki Sridévi Krishnan Nambyadi. To this gentleman I am indebted for the following further details on the snake-worship at Mannārsāla :—He says the name Mannārsāla means the 'unburnt ground.' This refers to an ancient tradition that when the great Khandavavanam was burnt by Agni, the god of fire, this small oasis was spared on the prayer of the serpents, who were the progeny of the serpent offspring of the lady of this Illam. As the Illam could not well accommodate the large number of the serpents that had multiplied, they were removed to a spot on the south of the house, where a magnificent grove has since been grown. In this spot are stone idols put up for the king and queen of snakes known as Nágarája and Nágayekshi, and for various members of the family which, according to my informant, number about 3,000. There are as many stone images in this grove now. In the cellar of the house, as well as in the grove where the stone images are placed, a solution of noorum palum is offered once a year, that is, on the day following the Sivarátri in the month of Mási. The same kind of offering is made to the Chittrakoodom also. About 12¼ Edangalies of dough and milk are mixed together and kept in the cellar. Thereafter the door of the cellar is shut for three days, and lest anybody pry into what passes within the cellar, the women of the household cover the crevices and holes of the door by the big cadjan umbrellas of the female inmates of the Illam. On the third day the door is opened, and whatever remains in the vessel of the dough and milk placed there is thrown into a tank as unfit for human use. The mixing up of noorum palum and the performing of the poojahs are done by the eldest female member of the Illam. The noorum palum is made of rice-flour, saffron powder, cow's milk, water of the tender cocoanut, fruit of the Kadali plantain, and ghee. In the Nálukettu of the house, offerings of noorum palum and cooked rice, as well as kuruthi (a red liquid composed of flour, saffron and chunam), take place every Ayilyam (star) day. Every morning the king and queen of serpents are washed, and an offering of fruit and milk is made to them; in the noon offerings of Vellanivedyam (cooked rice) and afterwards of fried grain (malar) follow. During the month of Kartika, a special poojah called navakom and offering of noorum palum are daily observed. On the Sivarátri day, in the month of Mási, the customary five poojahs and navakom are performed, and in the evening of the same day sacrificial offerings to the serpents and kuruti, as stated above, are made, and at the conclusion of the day's poojahs the idols are taken in procession round the temple. On Ayilyam (star) days, in the months of Purattási and Alpasi, all the serpent idols in the grove and the temples therein are taken in procession to the Illam, and offerings of noorum palum, kuruti and cooked rice are made there in propitiation of the serpent gods. The person who carries the idol of the Nágarája is the eldest female member of the Illam, and the procession is conducted with great pomp and rejoicings. According to my informant, the eldest female member of the house, though married, is expected to lead a celibate life when she becomes the oldest female in the family. During the festive days at Mannārsāla, about 5,000 people assemble to worship and propitiate the serpent gods, and their offerings include gold and silver coins, and gold, silver, copper or stone effigies of snakes, grains of all kinds, pepper, salt, saffron, tender cocoanuts, bunches of Kadali plantain, melons, oil, ghee, sandalwood, silk and other pilgrims. On the day previous to the Ayilyam ceremonial, about two or three thousand Brahmans are fed. The annual expense of this institution and worship at Mannārsāla is estimated at about 2,000 rupees. The kâvu has its own paddy fields and gardens, from the revenues of which it is maintained.

All the land about it, measuring a mile square, is said to belong to it. This would be enormous property, as the taluk where this kavoo is situated is one of the richest in Travancore. A trifle is given by the Sircar every year. If more funds are required, the Nambiyadi is expected to meet them from his own private income. The grove and its temples cover an immense oblong space measuring about 16 acres in extent. The inmates of the Illam are the poojaries of the gods in this grove. It is believed that whenever the poojah is not performed with the strictest personal purity or care to small details, the serpent gods get offended, which feeling is exhibited by the largest cobras coming out of the grove. It should be remembered that, as a rule, the serpents are not seen out of their holes, though hundreds of them are known to exist in these large groves. When any is seen, especially if a real cobra, the village astrologer is consulted, who readily finds out the cause of the wrath of the serpent gods, and steps are taken immediately to pacify them by propitiatory ceremonies. The people believe in these ceremonies most implicitly. That is not a mere form with them. In a house in North Travancore, where I lived some years, there used to be seen now and again snakes of all kinds, and in answer to my request to the servant of my landlord to keep the kavoo neat, he invariably said, "Please, sir, order some lights and milk to the kavoo," for this man most sincerely believed that this was the only effective way of keeping out the snakes from view. He did not seem to believe that there was any good in keeping the premises neat and clean. It should here be noted that a true Hindu population never pelt at or harm the snakes when they are seen. They are objects of worship. One of our retired officials told me that some years ago, when he was young and new to the place, he was puzzled by some of the parties present at his cutcherry telling him that the 'god was coming.' The crowd made way, and on rising, this official was horrified to see that the god referred to was a live cobra. This village he spoke of, even now abounds with serpents, but strange to say, these reptiles seldom harm man. They are evidently become domesticated animals, for we seldom hear of snake-bites in that village, though the general belief is that there are more snakes there than rats. The people also seem to be quite at home with them, for they do not get put out when they see these reptiles."

CUSTOMS, GAMES, FESTIVALS, ETC.

Hamilton in his "New Account of the East Indies" published in 1744, writes :—

"It was an ancient custom for the Samorin (Zamorin, then the local potentate) to reign but twelve years and no longer. If he died before his term was expired it saved him a trouble-some ceremony of cutting his own throat on a public scaffold erected for that purpose. He first made a feast for all his nobility and gentry, who were very numerous. After the feast, he saluted his guests, went on the scaffold, and very neatly cut his own throat in the view of the assembly. His body was, a little while after, burned with great pomp and ceremony, and the grandees elected a new Samorin. Whether that custom was a religious or a civil ceremony I know not, but it is now laid aside, and a new custom is followed by the modern Samorin, that a jubilee is proclaimed throughout his dominion, at the end of twelve years, and a tent is pitched for him in a spacious plain, and a great feast is celebrated for ten or twelve days with mirth and jollity, guns firing night and day, so at the end of the feast any four of the guests that have a mind to gain a crown by a desperate action in fighting their way through 30, or 40,000 of his guards, and kill the Samorin in his tent, he that kills him succeeds to him in his empire. In Anno 1695 one of these jubilees happened and the tent pitched near Ponnany (Ponani) a seaport of his about 16 leagues to the southward of Calicut. There were but three men that would venture on that desperate action, who fell on, with sword and target, among the guards, and after they had killed and wounded many were themselves killed. One of the *Desperadoes* had a nephew of fifteen or sixteen years of age, that kept close by his uncle in the attack on the guards, and when he saw him fall, the youth got through the guards into the tent and made a stroke at his majesty's head and had certainly dispatched him, if a large brass lamp which was burning over his head, had not marred the blow ; but before he could make another, he was killed by the guards ; and I believe the same Samorin reigns yet. I chanced to come that time along the coast and heard the guns for two or three days and nights successively."

Here must be made an excerpt from the "Malabar Manual" as its author Mr. Logan, while Collector (chief administrative officer) of Malabar, made excellent use of his opportunities to delve into the ancient archives of the district.

" The *Kêrala Mâhâtmya* so far corroborates Hamilton's story, that it declares the king used to be deposed at this festival, but there is no mention of self-immolation. although it is quite possible the deposed kings may have occasionally adopted this mode of escape from the chagrin of not being re-elected by their adherents." He goes on to say what Mr. Jonathan Duncan wrote about this festival, of which his account appears in the first volume of the Transactions of the Bombay Literary Society.

The festival was held last in 1743.

"Those who acknowledged the Zamorin's suzerainty sent flags in token of fealty; and the places where these flags used to be hoisted at festival times are still pointed out. The Valluvanād Raja, who is still represented in the management of the Tirunāvāyi temple by one of the four Brahman *Kārālars*, instead of sending a flag used to send men called *Chāvers* (men who have elected to die) whose office it was to endeavour to cut their way through the Zamorin's guards to his throne in a manner presently to be described. If they had succeeded in killing him—as on the occasion cited by Hamilton, whose statement except as to date, is moreover corroborated by tradition—it is uncertain what would have happened; but probably if a capable Raja had been ruling in Valluvanād at such a time, popular opinion would have endowed him with suzerainty, for the Nâyar militia were very fickle, and flocked to the standard of the man who was fittest to command and who treated them the most considerately.

"With the kind assistance of the present Zamorin, Maharaja Bahadur, the records of his family have been examined and a complete account obtained of the events attending the festival held in 1683 A.D., the festival next preceding that alluded to by Hamilton.

"The festival used to continue for twenty-eight days every twelfth year when the planet Jupiter was in retrograde motion in the sign of *Karkadagam* or Cancer or the Crab, and at the time of the eighth lunar asterism in the month of Makaram the festival used to culminate.

"On the occasion in question the Zamorin some months beforehand sent orders for the preparation of the necessary timber and bamboos for the temporary buildings required at *Tirunāvāyi* and the materials were floated down stream from the Aliparamba Chirakkal lands.

"Then exactly two months before the opening day he sent out a circular to his followers worded as follows :—

'Royal writing to the *Akampati Janam* (body-guards).

'On the 5th Makaram 858 is *Mahāmakha Talpuyam* (time of the eighth lunar asterism in the festival season), and the *Lōkars* (chief people of each locality) are required to attend at Tirunāvāyi as in olden times.

'Mangātt Raman and Tinayancheri are sent to collect and bring you in regular order for the Mahāmakham.'

"The Zamorin timed himself to arrive at Tirunāvāyi on the day after that appointed for the arrival of his followers, and the lucky moment for the setting out on this particular occasion on the last day's stage of the journey was at the rising of the constellation of Aquarius.

"The *Tirunāvāyi* temple stands on the north bank of the Ponnāni river close to the present line of railway. Passengers by train can catch a glimpse of it by looking across the level expanse of paddy-fields which lie south of the sixth telegraph post on the three hundred and eighty-second mile of the railway. There is a modest clump of trees on the river bank hiding the temple, the western gateway of which faces a perfectly straight piece of road a little over half a mile in length stretching from the temple gateway westwards to the elevated ridge hemming in the paddy-fields on the west. This road is but little raised above the level of the paddy flat. Directly facing this straight piece of road as the elevated ridge is reached there are three or perhaps four terraces, the outlines of which may still be traced in the face of the precipitous bank.

"A little to one side of the upper terrace are the ruins of a strongly built powder magazine, and on the flat ground above and on both sides of the fine avenue shading the public road at this place is ample space for the erection of temporary houses.

"In a neighbouring enclosure under cultivation is a disused well of fine proportions and of most solid construction.

"From the upper terrace alluded to a commanding view is obtained facing eastwards of the level rice-plain at foot, of the broad placid river on the right backed by low hills, of higher flat-topped laterite plateaus on the left, their lower slopes bosomed in trees, and, in the far distance, of the great chain of Western Ghâts with the Nilgiris in the extreme left front hardly distinguishable in their proverbial colour from the sky above them. It was on this spot, on a smooth plateau of hard laterite rock, raised some 30 to 40 feet above the plain, that the Zamorin used several times in the course of the festival to take his stand with the sword of Chēramān Perumāl, the last emperor, in his hand.

"The sword is and has been for centuries, slowly rusting away in its scabbard, but it is not alone on it that the Zamorin depends for his safety, for the plain below him is covered with the 30,000 Nâyars of Ernâd, the 10,000 of Polanâd and numberless petty dependent chieftains, each counting his fighting men by the hundred or the thousand or by thousands. Away on the right across the river are the camps of the second prince of the Zamorin's family and of the dependent Punnattūr Raja; the third, fourth, fifth, and sixth princes' camps too are close at hand in the left front behind the temple, and behind the terrace itself is the Zamorin's camp.

"The whole scene is being made gay with flags as an elephant is being formally caparisoned with a chain of solid gold with 'one hundred and fourteen small links and one clasp, making in all one hundred and fifteen'—as the record specifically testifies—and with golden bosses and other ornaments too numerous to be detailed. But this part of the ceremonies is not to be permitted to pass unchallenged, for it signifies in a formal manner the Zamorin's intention to assume the *rôle* of *Rakshapurashan* or protector of the festivities and of the people there assembled. On the instant, therefore, there is a stir among the crowd assembled near the western gate of the temple directly facing at half a mile distance the Zamorin's standing-place on the upper terrace.

"From this post, running due east in a perfectly straight line to the western gate of the temple, is the straight piece of road already described, but the road itself is clear and the armed crowd on the plain, it is seen, are hemmed in by barrel palisadings running the full length of the road on both sides. Two spears' length apart the palisades are placed, and the armed crowd on either hand, consisting on this occasion of the thirty thousand Ērnād Nāyars, it is seen, are all carrying spears. The spearmen may not enter that narrow lane, and by the mere weight of their bodies present an impossible obstacle to the free passage of the foemen now bent on cutting down the Zamorin in his pride of place.

"Amid much din and firing of guns the *morituri*, the *Chaver* Nāyars, the elect of four Nāyar houses in Valluvanād, step forth from the crowd and receive the last blessings and farewells of their friends and relatives. They have just taken of the last meal they are to eat on earth at the house of the temple representative of their chieftain; they are decked with garlands and smeared with ashes. On this particular occasion it is one of the houses of Putumanna Panikkar who heads the fray. He is joined by seventeen of his friends—Nāyar or Māppilla or other arms-bearing caste men—for all who so wish may fall in with sword and target in support of the men whe have elected to die.

"Armed with swords and targets alone they rush at the spearmen thronging the palisades; they 'winde and turn their Bodies, as if they had no Bones, casting them forward and backward, high and low, even to the Astonishment of the Beholders,' as worthy Master Johnson describes them in a passage already quoted (page 137). But notwithstanding the suppleness of their limbs, notwithstanding their delight and skill and dexterity in their weapons, the result is inevitable and is prosaically recorded in the chronicle thus: 'The number of *Chavers* who came and died early morning the next day after the elephant began to be adorned with gold trappings—being *Putumanna Kantur Menon* and followers—were 18.

"At various times during the ten last days of the festival the same thing is repeated. Whenever the Zamorin takes his stand on the terrace, assumes the sword and shakes it, men rush forth from the crowd at the west temple gate only to be impaled on the spears of the guardsmen who relieve each other from day to day. The turns for this duty are specifically mentioned in the chronicle thus: 'on the day the golden ornaments are begun to be used the body-guard consists of the thirty thousand; of Ellaya Vakkayil Vellōdi (and his men) the second day, of Netiyiruppu,* Mūttarāti Tirumulpād (and his men) the third day of Ittatūrnād,† Nambiyātiri Tirumulpād (and his men) the fourth day, of Ērnād Mūnāmkūr,‡ Nambiyātiri Tirumulpād (and his men) the fifth day, of Ērnād,§ Elankur Nambiyāttiri Tirumalpād (and his men) the sixth day, and of the ten thousand,|| the Calicut Talachanna Nāyar and Ērnād Mēnon the seventh day.'

"The chronicle is silent as to the turns for this duty on the eighth, ninth and tenth days. On the eleventh day, before the assembly broke up and after the final assault of the *Chāvers* had been delivered, the *Ernad Elankur Nambiyātiri Tirumalpad* (the Zamorin next in succession) and the *Tirumanisseri Nambūtiri* were conveyed in palanquins to the eastern end of the narrow palisaded lane, and thence they advanced on foot, prostrating themselves four times towards the Zamorin, once at the eastern end of the lane, twice in the middle, and once at the foot of the terraces. And after due permission was obtained they took their places on the Zamorin's right hand.

"After this, so the chronicle runs, it was the duty of the men who have formed the body guard to march up with music and pomp to make obeisance. On this occasion, however, a large portion of the body-guard seems to have been displeased, for they left without fulfilling this duty, and this story corroborates in a marked way the facts already set forth (page 132) regarding the independence and important political influence possessed by the Nāyars as a body.

"The *Ernād Menon* and the *Calicut Talachanna Nāyar* with their followers were the only chiefs who made obeisance in due form to the Zamorin on this occasion, and possibly by the time of the next festival (1695 A.D.), of which Hamilton wrote, the dissatisfaction might have increased among his followers and the Zamorin's life even may have been endangered

* The fifth Prince of the Zamorin's family.

† The fourth Prince of the Zamorin's family.

‡ The third Prince of the Zamorin's family.

§ The second Prince and heir apparent of the Zamorin's family.

|| The ten thousand of Pôlanād, the district round about Calicut, formed the Zamorin's own immediate body-guard—Conf. the account contained in the *Kēralolpatti* of how these men were originally selected — Chapter III, section (*a*).

as Hamilton alleges, probably through lack of men to guard him. Tradition asserts that the *Chāver* who managed on one occasion to get through the guards and up to the Zamorin's seat belonged to the family of the Chāndrattil Panikkar.

"The chronicle winds up with a list of the *Chāvers* slain on this occasion, viz.:—

When the Zamorin was taking his stand on the terrace apparently at the commencement of festivities	5
On the day the elephant was adorned as already stated	18
"The next day of *Chandrattil Panikkar* and followers, the number who came and died	11
'Of *Verkōt Panikkar* and followers the number that came and died the third day.	12
'The number who came to Vakkayūr and died in the four days	4
'The number of *Chāvers* who were arrested at the place where Kalattal Itti Karunākara Menon was, and brought tied to Vakkayūr and put to death	1
'The number of *Chāvers* arrested on the day of the sacrifice, when all the men together made the obeisance below Vakkayūr at the time when the Zamorin was taking his stand, and left tied to the bars, and who were afterwards brought to Vakkayūr and after the ceremony was over and the Zamorin had returned to the palace were put to the sword	4
Total ...	55

"The chronicle does not mention the fact, but a current tradition states that the corpses of the slain were customarily kicked by elephants as far as the brink of the fine well, of which mention has been made, and into which they were tumbled promiscuously. The well itself is nearly filled up with dêbris of sorts, and a search made at the spot would probably elicit conclusive evidence of the truth of this tradition.

"The martial spirit of the Nāyars was in former days kept alive by such desperate enterprises as the above, but in every-day-life the Nāyar used to be prepared and ready to take vengeance on any who affronted him, for he invariably carried weapons, and when a man was slain it was incumbent on his family to compass the death of a member of the slayer's family. This custom was called *kudippaka* (literally, *house feud*), or in an abbreviated form, *kuduppu*. One curious fact connected with this custom was that the chieftain of the district intervened when a man was slain, and the body of the deceased was by him taken to his enemy's house, and the corpse and the house were burnt together. It is understood that an out-house was usually selected for this purpose, but it was a common phrase to say—

'the slain rests in the yard of the slayer.'

"Again when mortal offence was given by one man to another, a solemn contract used to be entered into before the chieftain of the locality to fight a *duel*, the chieftain himself being the umpire. Large sums (up to a thousand fanams or two hundred and fifty rupees) used to be deposited as the battle-wager, and these sums formed one source (*ankam*) of the chieftain's revenue, and the right to levy them was sometimes transferred along with other privileges appertaining to the tenure of the soil. A preparation and training (it is said) for twelve years preceded the battle in order to qualify the combatants in the use of their weapons. The men who fought were not necessarily the principals in the quarrel—they were generally their champions. It was essential that one should fall, and so both men settled all their worldly affair before the day of combat."

The origin of the duo-decimal period is obscure, but to this day it obtains in Malabar (and in Malabar only) in relation to all agricultural affairs. The land, in contradistinction to the rest of the Presidency (as a rule), is the absolute property of the landholders—the whole of Malabar is; the landholders let out their land under certain conditions for periods of twelve years. This is the ordinary period of tenure; now a days, much of the land is leased informally on a yearly tenure. Tenants must renew their right to possession of their land every twelve years. The subject of land tenure in Malabar is a very extensive one, and we will not discuss it, resting satisfied with having noted the observance of the twelve yearly cycle in connection with it. It is supposed to be governed by the cycle of Jupiter.*

* Friar Jordanus, Bishop of Quilon in the 14th century, said that people make a vow, and to fulfil it cut off their own head before an idol. "Barbosa says that the king of Quilacne or Coliacaud (Calicut). . . . after reigning 12 years, always sacrificed himself to an idol in this way."—"Madras Manual of Administration," vol. iii, page 643.

The month Karkkatakam, when the Malayalis say "the body is cool," is the time when, according to custom, the Nâyar youths practise physical exercises. At Payôli in North Malabar, when I was there in August 1895, the local instructor of athletics was a Paravan, a mason by caste. As he had the adjunct 'Kurup' to his name it took some time to discover the fact. Teachers of his ilk are invariably of the Paravan caste, and when they are believed to be properly accomplished they are given the honorific 'Kurup.' So carefully are things regulated that no other person was permitted to teach athletics within the amshom (a local area, a small county): and his women folk had privileges, they only being the midwives who could attend on the Nâyar women of the amshom. His fee for a course of exercises for the month was ten rupees. He and some of his pupils gave an exhibition of their quality.

Besides bodily contortions and somersaults (practised in a long low-roofed shed having a sandy floor) there is play with the following instruments:—"Waṭṭa" (as in the illustration) "cheruvadi," a short stick, and a stick like a quarter staff called a sarîravadi—"stick the length of one's body." The waṭṭa is held in the right hand as a dagger; it is used to stab or strike and, in some ingenious way turn over an opponent. The total length of the waṭṭa is two feet, and of the cheruvadi about three feet. The latter is squared at the ends and is but a short staff.

It is held in the right hand a few inches from the end, and is used for striking and guarding only. The sarîravadi is held at or near one end by one or by both hands; the distance between the hands is altered constantly, and so is the end of the stick, which is grasped now by one now by another end by either hand as occasion may require; sometimes it is grasped in the middle. The performance with these simple things was astonishing. I should say the waṭṭa and the cheruvadi represented swords, or rather that they were used for initiation or practice in swordmanship when the Nâyars were the military element in Malabar. The opponents who faced each other with the sarîravadi or quarter staff, stood 30 feet apart, and, as if under the same stimulus, each kicked one leg high in the air, a la cancan, gave several lively bounds in the air, held their staff horizontally in front with outstretched arms, came down *slowly* on the haunches, placed the staff on the ground, bent over and touched it with the forehead. With a sudden bound they were again on their feet, and after some preliminary pirouetting went for each other tooth and nail.

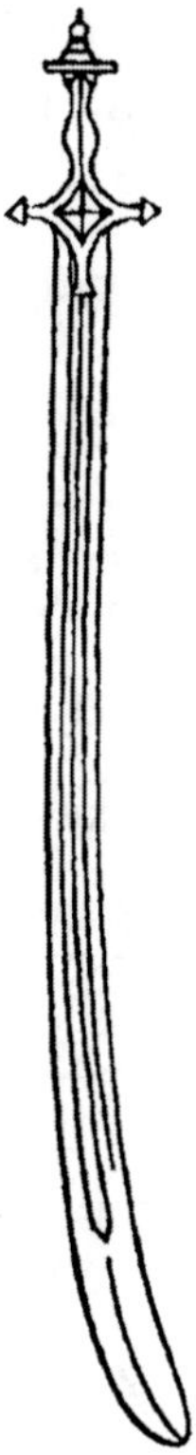

The sword play which one sees during festive ceremonies, a marriage or the like, done by the hereditary retainers who fight imaginary foes and destroy and vanquish opponents with much contortion of body, always indulge in much of this preliminary overture to their performance. There is always, by way of preliminary, a high kick in the air, followed by squatting on the haunches, bounding high, turning, twisting, pirouetting, and all the time swinging the sword unceasingly above, below, behind the back, under the arm or legs—in ever so many impossible ways.

Nâyar swords and shields are figured in the illustration. The shields are made of wood covered with leather, usually coloured bright red. Within the boss are some hard seeds, or metal balls loose in a small space, so that there is a jingling sound like that of the small bells on the ankles of the dancer, when the shield is oscillated or shaken in the hand. The swords are those which were used ordinarily for fighting. There are also swords of many patterns for processional and other purposes, more or less ornamented about the handle and half way up the blade ; but the one which is figured will suffice to show what the Nâyar fighting sword was like. The smaller shields are now used in play.

THE ÔNAM FESTIVAL.

The popular festival of Malabar is the Ônam, occurring in the last days of August or early in September. It is the great occasion for general rejoicing, when every one gives and receives presents, when the children are to be seen roaming everywhere gathering flowers, to make the flower carpets which are a distinctive feature of this happy season. For the Ônam is not merely a one-day festival. It lasts three days at least, and the ten days preceding it are occupied in preparations and in games—Ônam games. A writer (a Malayali evidently), in the "Calcutta Review" for January 1899, thus describes the Ônam season:—

"There are a great many of these Ônam ballads; but most of them are of a piece with the specimen given. It is a delight to hear them chanted in the early morning hours by bands of light-hearted children with clear bell-like voices ;—

Chembil house maiden, little maiden,
What did he give you who yesterday came ?
A new dress he gave me, a small dress he gave me,
A lounge likewise on which to recline,
A tank to disport in, a well to draw water from, a compound To gambol in, a big field to sing in.
Freshen up flowers, oh freshen for me.
On the south and the north shore, in the compound of Kannan, there grew up and flourished a thumba flower plant.
Out of this plant were fifty boats gotten ; at the head of each boat a banyan tree grew.
From the banyan there grew a tiny little babe, and a drum and a stick for the baby to play with.
The drum and the drum-stick, the household domestic, all together they flew away and they vanished.
Freshen up, flowers, oh freshen for me.
A measure and a half measure, and elephant's chains and earrings, who goes under the flower tree beneath which the elephant passes ?
It is no one at all, it is no one at all ; it is the Kuttikat baby god ; when we went forth to pluck of ripe fruit, a mischievous urchin sprang up and bit us.
With bitten foot when we went to the Brahmin's, the Brahmin lady, we found, had been injured.
With bitten foot then we went to the house of Edathil, whose lady with fever lay stricken.
Freshen up, flowers, oh freshen for me.

At noon of Attam day a bamboo fresh sprouted, and therewith we made us a good fish trap.

And when to the tank a fishing we went, we baited a minnow.

By its tail did we hold it, on the *bund* did we dash it, and of cocoanuts, with milk full, eighteen we ground.

With elephant pepper we dressed it; with asafœtida we filled it, right up to the elephant's head.

Freshen up, flowers, oh freshen for me.

Having set out at dawn to gather blossoms, the little children return with their beautiful spoils by 9 or 10 A.M.; and then the daily decorations begin. The chief decoration consists of a carpet made out of the gathered blossoms, the smaller ones being used in their entirety, while the large flowers and one or two varieties of foliage of differing tints are pinched up into little pieces to serve the decorator's purpose. This flower carpet is invariably made in the centre of the clean strip of yard in front of the neat house. Often it is a beautiful work of art accomplished with a delicate touch and a highly artistic sense of tone and blending. Among the flowers that contribute to the exquisite design may be named the common red, as well as the rarer variegated, lantana, the large red shoe flower *(Hibiscus rosa sinensis)* an indispensable feature of the cultivated vegetation in a Malayali's homestead, the yellow marigold, the yellow aster, the scarlet button flower, the sacred *tulsi (Ocimum sanctum)*, the wee, modest *thumber* (a vermifugal member of the Nepetæ tribe), the common *tagara* (yellow wild Cassia), the beautiful bluebell, and another common species of Cassia which the natives call the "Ônam flower." In addition, various little violet and purple wildlings that adorn the margins of rice fields, and beautiful specimens of the lily and allied orders of tropical plants are requisitioned by the weavers of these remarkably handsome, but, alas, quickly perishable, carpets. The carpet completed, a miniature pandal, hung with little festoons, is erected over it, and at all hours of the day neighbours look in, to admire and criticise the beautiful handiwork. This object is peculiar to the naturally well favoured province of Kéralam; and it serves to remind us that the people who possess the refined taste to produce such a pretty work of art must have long enjoyed a very high order of civilisation."

It has been noticed already under description of Nambûtiri Brahmans (Bulletin, Vol. III, No. 1), that the cloths given as "Ônam presents" are yellow, or some part of them is yellow. There must be at least a yellow stripe or a small patch of yellow in a corner, which suggests a relic of sunworship in a form more pronounced than that which obtains at present. It is a harvest festival, about the time when the first crop of paddy is harvested. As a rule the Ônam season is one of bright sunshine following the almost continuous rain of June, July and August.

I once witnessed a very interesting game called êitû (êiththu), played by the Nâyars in the Southern portion of Kurumbranâd during the ten days preceding Ônam. Curiously, the locality and the period are, so to speak, fixed. There is a semi-circular stop-butt, about two feet in the highest part, the centre, and sloping to the ground at each side. The players stand 25 to 30 yards before the concave side of it, one side of the players to the right, the other to the left. There is no restriction of numbers as to "sides." Each player is armed with a little bow made of bamboo about 18 inches in length, and artows or what answer for arrows, these being no more than pieces of the midrib of the cocoanut palm leaf, roughly broken off, leaving a little bit of the leaf at one end to take the place of the feather. In the centre of the stop-butt, on the ground, is placed the target, a piece of the heart of the plantain tree, about 3 inches in diameter, pointed at the top, in which is stuck a small stick convenient for lifting the "cheppu" as the mark which is the immediate objective of the players is called. They shoot indiscriminately at the mark, and he who hits it (the little arrows shoot straight and stick in readily) carries of all the arrows lying on the ground. Each "side" strives to secure all the arrows and to deprive the other side of theirs. A sort of "beggar my neighbour." He who hits the mark *last* takes all the arrows; that is, he who hits it, and runs and touches the mark before any one else hits it. As I stood watching, it happened several times that as many as four arrows hit the mark, while the youth who had hit it first was running the 25 yards to touch the "cheppu." Before he could touch it, as many as four other arrows had struck it; and, of course, he who hit it last and touched the mark secured all the arrows for his side. The game is accompanied by much shouting, gesticulation, and laughter. Those returning after securing a large number of arrows turned somersaults, and in saltatory motions expressed their joy.

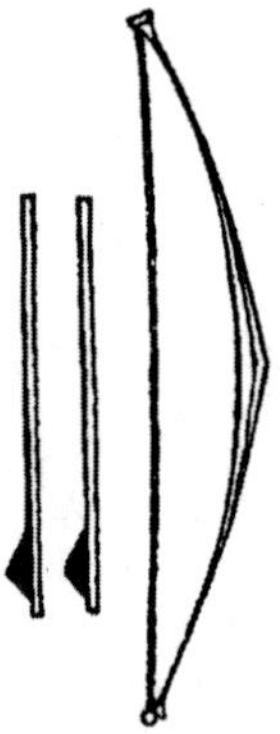

In the south-east of Malabar, in the neighbourhood of Palghat, the Ônam games are of a rougher character, the tenants of certain jenmis (landlords) turning out each under their own leader, and engaging in sham fights in which there is much rough play. Here, too, is to be seen a kind of boxing which would seem to be a relic of the days of the Roman pugiles using the cestus in combat. The position taken up by the combatants is much the same as that of the pugiles. The Romans were familiar with Malabar from about 30 B.C. to the decline of their power. We may safely assume that the "3,000 lbs. of pepper" which Alarie demanded as part of the ransom of Rome when he besieged the city in the fifth century, came from Malabar.*

Before ending this very incomplete account of customs of the Nâyars, mention must be made of two more of these, both odd. Ever since ChârAman Perumal departed from the west coast of India in A.D. 825, setting sail for Arabia and Mecca, having divided up his kingdom, His Highness the Maharajah of Travancore when ascending his throne says: "I ascend the musnud, and will rule until my uncle returns." The "uncle" is Châraman Perumal, the last sovereign of the west coast, who, having embraced the Muhammadan religion which was brought to his shores by Arab traders, proceeded to carry out a wild idea—so goes the legend—of receiving instruction from the Prophet himself! He never returned. To one princeling was given the territory now known as Travancore, and his surviving successor (through the female line of course) is the present Maharajah of Travancore. To another he gave Cochin, the ruler of which State also inherits through the female line. To the ancestor of the Zamorin of Calicut the Perumal gave no territory, as to the others, but he gave him his sword (it is still in existence) with the advice "to die and kill and annex." That he annexed is quite clear, as he was the sovereign not only of Calicut but of the country round about when modern Europeans first visited the west coast of India. Like the Maharajah of Travancore, the Zamorin repeats the formula that he rules until his uncle returns, but in his case it forms part of an elaborate and costly ceremony. The fort, which was the official residence of the Zamorin,

* See Madras Government Museum Catalogue No. 2, Roman Coins, by Mr. Edgar Thurston, Superintendent of the Museum.

was in Calicut,* and it has always been necessary for the new Zamorin to come to this fort in Calicut in a very formal manner. The residences, the kôvilagams of the various branches of the family, lie far to the eastward. The heir to the Zamorinship must make his formal entry into Calicut, for until he does so he is not, strictly speaking, the Zamorin. There is much obscurity as to details of the ceremonial, and I have not been able to note these satisfactorily, so will state merely so much as is undoubtedly correct. The new Zamorin comes to the bank of the Kallai river adjoining Calicut. There he is asked some questions, and he crosses this river in a *boat*—not over the bridge. Arrived on the Calicut side he must partake of some betel-leaf from a Mâppila man dressed as a (Mâppila) woman, or, as some say, from a Mâppila woman† and he says that he assumes the title of Zamorin and rules until his uncle returns. The betel-leaf, received from a (Muhammadan) Mâppila, which he chews, defiles him. He has lost his status in the caste, and he is supposed to be henceforth celibate. It would seem that this old world ceremony is likely to follow the track along which so much of what is interesting in India is disappearing. The late Zamorin never went through it, and he was therefore never, properly speaking, the Zamorin. He held the title perfunctorily, and he was the kârnavan of the immense property of the family; but he could not go "in procession" as Zamorin.‡ There are three unpleasant concomitants to the ceremony. It costs much money. It involves degradation in caste. It compels chastity.

The other odd custom is not one affecting merely an individual and a few with him, but it is a sexual one, and

---

* There is now no sign of it, though the site is known.

† Those who say that a woman gives the betel-leaf say, very reasonably, that a Mâppila man would never for any consideration or purpose wear a woman's garb. But, on the other hand, it is said the person *is* and must be a man, and that he dresses for this occasion only, as a woman.

‡ The Zamorin was in Calicut but once since he became Zamorin on the occasion of his visit to His Excellency the Governor of Madras in 1896, and then infringed custom by coming to Calicut without previously undergoing the ceremony. Owing to a death in the family he was under pollution and therefore unable to undertake the ceremony at that time, so he came by train. These old-fashioned customs, written or unwritten, take no count of trains. For example, the modern pilgrims from Northern India find the train very convenient when they wish to visit Rameshvaram. The penance of a life is reduced to a few days in a train. What would the old sages say! So the Zamorin came by train. But he could not go "in procession" along the road *as Zamorin*, and was obliged to make his visit as an ordinary grandee.

therefore one belonging to the community at large—in South Malabar, at any rate. The system of inheritance through females as it obtains amongst the Nâyars, relieves the woman from that undignified position which she occupies throughout the civilized world as the personal chattel of her husband. It gives her a relative superiority, and she carries this elsewhere. Coitus haud ita fit ut supina mulier viro morem gerat, immo etiam supino viro insidens illa, facie in eum conversâ genibusgue hic atqus illic dispositis negotium illud perficere solet. Hanc veneris figuram feminis ineundiorem, atque idcirco ab iis vindicatam esse perhibent periti. The well-known *jape* by which Iago hoped to arouse Brabantio into activity would be altogether inapplicable here.

Two more excerpts from Mr. Gopal Panniker's little book will be made, with his permission, descriptive of the other two most important national or popular festivals of Malabar.

"THE VISHU FESTIVAL.

"Vishu, like the Onam and the Thiruvathira Festivals, is a remarkable event amongst us. Its duration is limited to one day. The 1st of Mêtam (some day in April) is the unchangeable day on which it falls. It is practically the Astronomical New Year's Day.* This was one of the periods when in olden days the subjects of ruling princes or authorities in Malabar under whom their lots were cast, were expected to bring their New Year's offerings to such princes. Failure to comply with the said customary and time-conscerated demands was visited with royal displeasure resulting in manifold varieties of oppression. The British Government finding this was a great burden pressing rather heavily upon the people, obtained as far back as 1790, a binding promise from those Native Princes that such exactions of presents from the people should be discontinued thereafter. Consequently it is now shorn of much of its ancient sanctity and splendour. But suggestive survivals of the same are still to be found in the presents (explained further on) which tenants and dependants bring to leading families on the day previous to the Vishu.

"Being thus the commencement of a New Year, native superstition surrounds it with a peculiar solemn importance. It is believed that a man's whole prosperity in life depends upon

* See Madras Museum Bulletin, Vol. III, No. 1, pp. 57 and 58.

the nature, auspicious or otherwise, of the first things that he happens to fix his eyes upon on this particular morning. According to Nair and even general Hindu Mythology there are certain objects which possess an inherent inauspicious character. For instance ashes, firewood, oil and a lot of similar objects are inauspicious ones which will render him who chances to notice them first fare badly in life for the whole year, and their obnoxious effects will be removed only on his seeing holy things, such as, reigning princes, oxen, cows, gold and such like ones on the morning of the next New Year. Whereas wholesome and favourable consequences can be produced by the sight of auspicious objects like those just enumerated. The effects of the sight of these various materials are said to apply even to the attainment of objects by a man starting on a special errand who happens for the first time to look at them after starting. However, with this view, almost every family religiously takes care to prepare the most sight-worthy objects on the New Year morning. Therefore, on the previous night they prepare what is known, in native phraseology, as a *kani*. A small circular bell-metal vessel is taken and some holy objects are systematically arranged inside it. A Grandha or old book made of palmyra leaves, a gold ornament, a new-washed clothe, some "unprofitably gay" flowers of the *Konna* tree, a measure of rice, a so-called looking-glass made of bell-metal, and a few other things, are all tastefully arranged in the vessel and placed in a prominent room inside the house. On either side of this vessel two brass or bell-metal lamps filled with cocoanut oil "clear as diamond sparks" are kept intensely burning and a small plank of wood or some other seat is placed in front of it. At about 5 o'clock in the morning of the day some one who has got up first wakes up the inmates, both male and female, of the house and takes them blindfolded so that they may not gaze at anything else, to the seat near the Kani. The members are seated one after another in the seat and are then and not till then asked to open their eyes and carefully look at this Kani. Then each is made to look at some venerable member of the house or sometimes a stranger even. This over, the little playful urchins of the house begin to fire small crackers which they have bought and stored for the occasion. The Kani is then taken round the place from house to house for the benefit of the poor families, which cannot afford to prepare such a costly adornment. With the close of the carelessly confused noise of the crackers the morning breaks and preparations are begun for the morning meal. This meal is in some parts confined to rice-kanji with a grand appendage of other eatable substances and in others to ordinary rice and its accompaniments, but in either case on grand scales.

"Immediately the day dawns the heads of the families give to almost all the junior members and servants of the household and to wives and children, money-presents varying from 4 as. to a rupee or two. Children preserve these presents to serve as their pocket money. In the more numerically large families similar presents are also made by the heads of particular branches of the same family to their juniors, children, wives and servants. These presents are intended to be the forerunners of incomes to them more splendid all the year round.

"But one other item connected with the festival deserves mention. On the evening of the previous day, about four or five o'clock most well-to-do families distribute paddy or rice, as the case may be, in varying quantities with some other accessories to the family-workmen, whether they live on the family-estates or not. In return for this, these labourers bring with them for presentation the fruits of their own labours such as vegetables of divers sorts, cocoanut oil, jaggery, plantains, pumpkins, cucumbers, brinjals, &c., in ways such as their respective circumstances might permit.

"With the close of the noon-meal the festival practically concludes, and nothing remains of it for the next day or for the same evening, for that matter. In some families after the noon-meals are over, dancing and games of various kinds are carried on, which contribute to the enhancement of the pleasantries incidental to the festival. As on other prominent occasions, card-playing and other games are also resorted to."

"THE THIRUVATHÎRA FESTIVAL.

"Thiruvathira is one of the three great national occasions of Malabar. It generally comes off in the Malayalam month of Dhanu (December or January) on the day called the Thiruvathira day. It is essentially a festival in which females are almost exclusively concerned and lasts for but a single day. The popular conception of it is that it is in commemoration of the death of Kamadevan, the Cupid of our national mythology. As recorded in the old Puranas, Kamadevan was destroyed in the burning fire of the third eye of Siva, one of the chief members of our Divine Trinity. Hence he is now supposed as having only an ideal or rather spiritual existence, and thus he exerts a powerful influence upon the lower passions of human nature. The memory of this unhappy tragedy is still kept alive amongst us, particularly the female section, by means of the annual celebration of this important festival. About a week before the day, the festival practically opens. At about 4 in the morning every young female member of Nair families with pretensions to decency, gets out of her bed and takes her bath in a tank. Usually, a fairly large number of these young ladies collect themselves in the tank for the purpose. Then all or almost all of these plunge in the water and begin to take part in the singing that is presently to follow. One of these then leads off by means of a peculiar rhythmic song chiefly pertaining to Cupid. This singing is simultaneously accompanied by a curious sound produced with her hand on the water. The palm of the left hand is closed and kept immediately underneath the surface of the water. Then the palm of the other is forcibly brought down in a slanting direction and struck against its surface. So that the water is completely ruffled and is splashed in all directions producing a loud deep noise. This process is continuously prolonged together with the singing. One stanza is now over along with the sound and then the leader stops a while for the others to follow her in her wake. This being likewise over, she caps her first stanza, with another at the same time beating on the water and so on until the conclusion of the song. Then all of them make a long pause and then begin another. The process goes on until the peep of dawn when they rub themselves dry and come home to dress themselves in the neatest and grandest possible attire. They also darken the fringes of their eyelids with a sticky preparation of soot mixed up with a little oil or ghee; and sometimes with a superficial coating of antimony powder. They also wear white, black, or red marks lower down the middle of their foreheads close to the part where the two eyebrows near one another. They also chew betel and thus redden their mouths and lips. Then they proceed to the enjoyment of another prominent item of pleasure, viz., swinging to and fro, on what is usually known as an Uzhinjal.*

"On the festival day after the morning bath is over, they take a light meal and in the noon the family-dinner is voraciously attacked; the essential and almost universal ingredients of which being ordinary ripe plantain fruits and a delicious preparation of arrow-root powder purified and mixed with jaggery or sugar and also cocoanut. Then till evening dancing and merry-making are ceaselessly indulged in.

"The husband population are inexcusably required to be present in the wives' houses before evening as they are bound to do on the Onam and Vishu occasions; failure to do which is looked upon as a step or rather the first step on the part of the defaulting husband towards a final separation or divorce from the wife. Despite the rigour of the bleak December season during which commonly the festival falls, heightened inevitably by the constant blowing of the cold east wind upon their moistened frames, these lusty maidens derive considerable pleasure from their early baths and their frolics in water. The biting cold of

* A swing made of bamboo.

the season which makes their persons shiver and quiver like aspen-leaves before the breeze, becomes to them in the midst of all their ecstatic frolics an additional source of pleasure. In short, all these merely tend to brace them up to an extent the like of which they can scarcely find anywhere else.

"The two items described above, viz., the swinging process and the beating on the water, have each its own distinctive significance. The former typifies the attempt which these maidens make in order to hang themselves on these instruments and destroy their lives in consequence of the lamented demise of their sexual deity, Kamadevan. It is but natural that depth of sorrow will lead men to extreme courses of action. The beating on the water symbolizes their beating their chests in expression of their deep-felt sorrow caused by their Cupid's death. Such in brief is the description of a Nair festival which plays a conspicuous part in the social history of Malabar."

Mr. Gopal Pannikar's chapter on "Local Traditions and Superstitions" ("Malabar and its Folk") has special value, for in it he recounts existing popular belief. He tells us that to demon labourers are attributed the existence of old dilapidated wells and buildings, demons who perform Herculean tasks under orders of a chief. One day these demons having finished their task disturbed their chief when he was playing a game of chess, coming to ask for more work, so he told them to count the waves of the sea; and this is why they are still at work. He tells us why the crow has a long life and the fowl a short one, and how that the former has but one eye, rolling in a socket; how it is that the common squirrel is marked on the back by the fingers of Vishnu; and much that is of interest about the screech owl, the lizard, the crocodile, and many other things. He recalls to my mind the popular belief accounting for the unluckiness which will follow should one see the moon on the Chadûrti night, which I have heard in North Malabar. My note was somehow mislaid. It is that the big-bellied god Ganapati was once upon a time returning home in the moonlight after a repast so generous that his person was much distended, and unable to see his feet, he tripped and stumbled. He looked around to see whether any one had observed his discomfiture. There was no one but the moon. The moon laughed, whereupon he cursed the moon. Hence the belief that whoever sees the moon on that night will be unlucky, probably defamed. Mr. Gopal Panniker, a native of South Malabar, does not mention it, but in North Malabar women are scrupulously careful not to see the moon or be for a moment in the moonlight during that night for fear of calumny. There, the men do not care much. We will now bid adieu to Mr. Gopal Pannikar, but not without thanking him for all he has told us about his own people.

Uchâl (Uchaval) is the term used for the first three days of the Malayalam month Makaram, usually falling between the 15th and 20th January. All over Malabar, with the exception of Wynâd, above the ghâts, there are two crops of rice every year, one with the south-west, one with the north-east monsoon. Elsewhere in Southern India rice land is always irrigated, but in Malabar there is no such thing, practically, as irrigation, the heavy rainfall rendering it unnecessary, and the earth goddess—Bhûmi Dêvi—brings forth her fruit under the stimulus of the rain from heaven. She produces the crops as a female produces her children, and from the 1st of the month Makaram, she rests until the cultivator again begins to disturb her, three months later, when the showers preceding the south-west monsoon fall. Uchâl is the period of three days when the earth goddess menstruates. Granaries and all receptacles of grain are closed during Uchâl—they are not even visited. Paddy is not sold. No implement of cultivation is touched. The rice to be used during the three days is pounded out beforehand and kept separate. But it is no season of gloom; rather is it one of festivity. As particular forms of food partaken on specific occasions have an interest of their own, we must not omit description of the Uchâl cake—the Pâla Ata. (Pâla—spathe of the areca-palm, Ata—cake). A paste is made of rice flour and water and spread thickly (about an inch thick) on one side of two pieces of the spathe of the areca-palm, each piece being from 2 to 3 feet in length and about 8 inches wide. Powdered jaggery, scraped cocoanut, powdered ginger, a little garlic and other condiments, are then put in small quantities on the paste. The two pieces of the spathe are then placed together, and they are stitched all round the edges. The whole is covered over with soft red mud and put into a fire where it is kept until the mud covering cracks. The cake is then cooked and ready for eating. It is cut and distributed to members of the family and friends.

In parts of Malabar the Tîyan tenants present these cakes to their Nâyar landlords as a token of allegiance or submission. Rice is the only article of food which if prepared by a Tîyan the Nâyar cannot eat; so the Nâyar has no caste scruples about eating the Pâla Ata prepared for him by the Tîyan at Uchâl. I recollect a case of murder which arose out of nothing more or less than a Tîyan tenant's refusal to present his Nâyar landlord with a Pâla Ata at Uchâl. I once tried to preserve one of these cakes, but the results were too disastrous for description.*

HABITATIONS.

A house may face east or west; never north or south. As a rule the Nâyar's house faces the east. Every garden is enclosed by a bank, a hedge, or a fencing of some kind, and entrance is to be made at one point only, the east, where there is a gate-house, or, as in the case of of the poorest houses a small portico, or open doorway roofed over. One never walks straight through this; there is always a kind of stile to surmount. It is the same everywhere in Malabar, and not only amongst the Nâyars. The following is a plan of a nâlupura or four-sided house, which may be taken as representative of the houses of the rich:

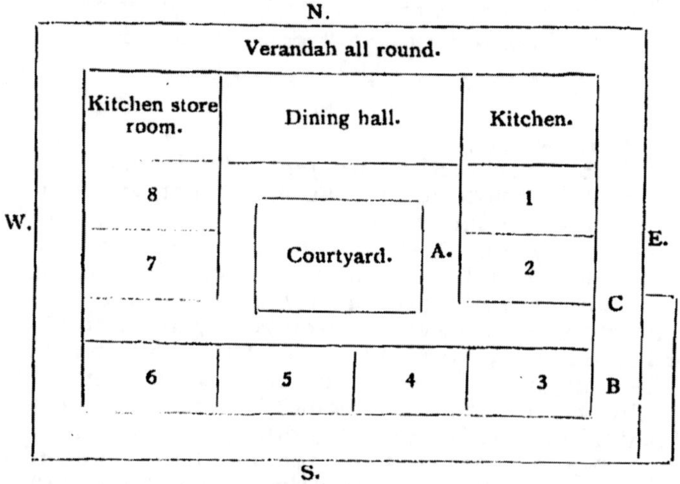

Numbers 6 and 7 are rooms which are used generally for storing grain.

At A is a staircase leading to the room of the upper story occupied by the female members of the family. At B is a staircase to the rooms of the upper story

*For much of the information regarding Uchâl I am indebted to Mr. M. Raman Menon.

occupied by the male members. There is no connection between the portions allotted to the men and that of the women. No. 8 is for the family gods. The Kârnavans and old women of the family are perpetuated in images of gold or silver, or, more commonly, brass. Poor people, who cannot afford to make these images, substitute simply a stone. Offerings are made to these images (or to the stones) at every full moon. The throat of a fowl will be cut outside, and the bird is then taken inside and offered.

The entrance is at C.

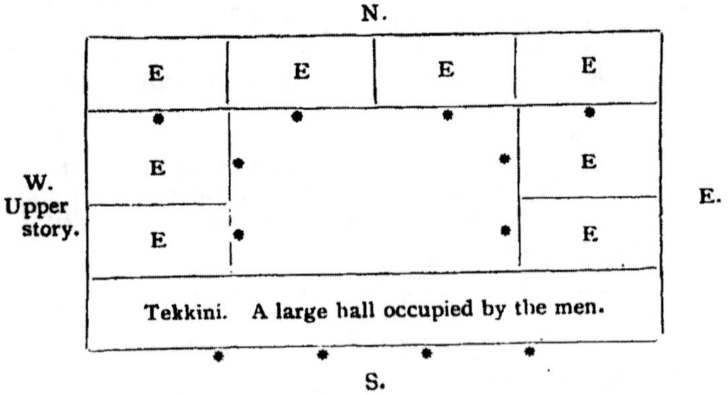

Windows at * * * *

E. Rooms occupied by women and children.

It may be noticed that the apartment, where the men sleep, has no windows on the side of the house which is occupied by the women. The latter are relatively free from control by the men as to who may visit them. We saw, when speaking of funeral ceremonies, that a house was supposed to have a central courtyard; and of course it has this only when there are four sides to the house. The nâlupura, or four-sided house, is the proper one for in this alone can all ceremonial be observed in orthodox fashion. But it is not the ordinary Nâyar's house that

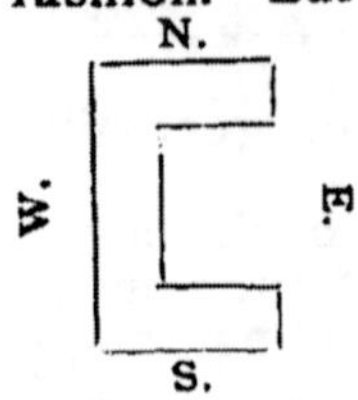

one sees all over Malabar. The ordinary house is, roughly, of the shape here indicated. Invariably there is an upper story. There are no doors but only a few tiny windows opening to the west. Men sleep in one end, women in the other, each having their own staircase. Around the house there is always shade from many trees and palms. Every house is in its own seclusion.

ASTROLOGY, MAGIC,* WITCHCRAFT.

Astrology.—The ordinary astrologer of Malabar is a man of the Kanisan or Panikkar † caste, a community relatively low in the social scale, therefore carrying pollution to those of the higher caste. A curious position in society for people of a learned profession to occupy. The Panikkar is also, very often, the schoolmaster. He is in request in connection with every social function, religious or other, and of course, at every birth. His astrology, he will tell you, is divided into three parts:

(1) Ganîta, which treats of the constellations;
(2) Samkîta, which explains the origin of the constellations, comets, falling stars, earthquakes;
(3) Hôra, by which the fate of man is explained.

The Panikkar, who follows in the foot-steps of his forefathers, should have a thorough knowledge of astrology and of mathematics, and be learned in the Vêdas. He should be sound in mind and body, truthful and patient. He should look well after his family, and he should worship regularly the nine planets:—Sûryan—the Sun; Chandran—Moon; Chovva—Mars; Bûdhan—Mercury; Vyâzham, or Guru, or Brihaspati—Jupiter; Sukran, or Sani—Venus; Râhu and Kêtu. The two last, though not visible, are, oddly enough, classed as planets by the Panikkar. They are said to be two parts of an Âsura who was cut in two by Vishnu.

I here reproduce a diagram made for me by a Panikkar showing the relative positions of the planets on the 7th of April 1895:

Sûryan, Bûdhan.	Sukkran.	Chovva.	Brihaspati.
Râhu.			
			Kêtu.
		Sani.	Chandran.

N.B.—Chandran remains 2¼ days in each of the 12 *rasis* or celestial chambers.

* What was said under "Magic and sorcery" when describing Nambûtiri Brahmans, Bulletin, Vol. III, No. I, applies also to the Nâyar.

† This is not to be confounded with the honorific Panikkar affixed to the name of a Nâyar.

The Panikkars dabble also in magic. In Plates XVI, XVII are figured four yantrams, selected from a number in my possession as representative, presented to me by a Panikkar. They should be written on a thin gold, silver or copper plate (a yantram written on gold is the most effective), and worn on the person. As a rule, the yantram is placed in a little cylindrical case made of silver, fastened to a string tied round the waist. Many of these are often worn by the same person. The yantram is sometimes written on cadjan or paper. I have one of this kind in my collection taken from the neck of a goat. It is common to see them worn on the arm, or round the neck.

No. I. Aksharamâla.—Fifty-one letters. Used in connection with every other yantram. Each letter has its own meaning, and does not represent any word. In itself this yantram is powerless; but it gives life to all others. It must be written on the same plate as the other yantram.

No. II. Sûlini.—For protection against sorcery, or devils. This is to invoke the goddess and secure her aid. The ceremony brings a blessing to the receiver of the charm.

No. III. Mâha Sûlini.—To be used to prevent all kinds of harm through devils, chief of whom is Pulatini—he who eats infants. May be used also as protective against enemies. Women wear it to avert miscarriage. The letter in the middle, Hûm Mâha Sûlini. That in the rim is Om.

No. IV. Kâla Bhâiravi.—Represents the goddess. The goddess must be pleased *first* by worship. No sacrifice, which is rather odd, as this terrible goddess is generally represented in Southern India as loving blood. The letters do not form any mantram. Each letter has life in itself. Prevents all harm from enemies, and attack by devils.

Other yantrams to be used in much the same way as these are:—

The *Ganapati* yantram. To increase knowledge. To put away fear and shyness.

The *Sarasvati* yantram. To enable its possessor to please his listeners, and increase his knowledge.

The *Panchakshari* yantram, a square containing 81 smaller squares, in each a mystic letter; the whole representing Siva. For persons on whom medicines have no effect. Also against evil spirits. A person out of whom an evil spirit has been driven is perfectly safe ever after with this carried on his person.

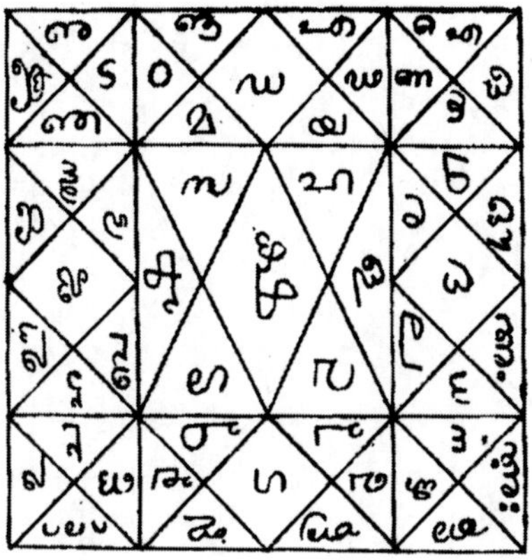

I

II

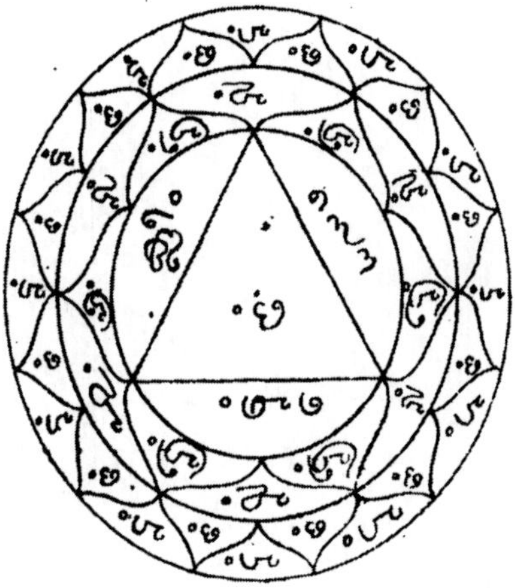

III

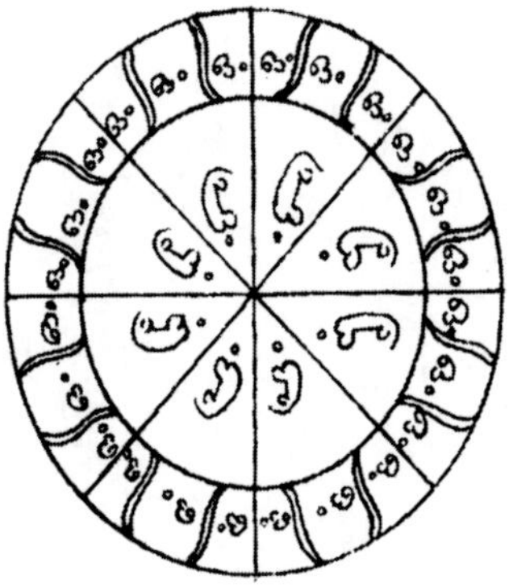

IV

Reg: No. 1425 & 26
Copies 200

Zinco., Survey Office, Madras.
1915

The *Santâna gôpâlam* yantram. As a whole, it represents Sri Krishna. The letters in it (there are 101) put together in a certain way form a mantram. It is used by barren women so that they may bear children. It may be traced on a metal plate and worn in the usual way, or on a slab of butter which is then eaten. When the latter method is adopted it is repeated on 41 successive days, during which the woman as well as the Panikkar may not have sexual connection.

The *Srî Sûkra* yantram is another used by childless men and women in order to obtain offspring. The others are prophylactic against evil spirits (chiefly), to defeat enemies, to succeed in all undertakings and prevent loss of property by theft, to win over the good feeling of others, and so on. The *Sudarsana* yantram not only relieves sickness, but when drawn in 5 colours on the ground and worshipped while repeating a mantram (too long to quote) wards off the evil influence caused through black magic! Another, the *Navva* yantram, drawn in ashes of cowdung on a new cloth which is then tied round the waist, relieves a women in labour. Yet another, the *Asvârûdha* yantram (Asva, horse ; ârûḍha, to climb) would also be useful to some people, as a person wearing it is able to cover long distances easily on horseback ; and he may make the most refractory horse amenable by tying it round its neck. It will also help to cure sick cattle. In some the letters or syllables form a distinct mantram, while in others each has its own mystic meaning.

Let me hasten to assure any one desirous of applying one of these charms to himself that they are entirely inoperative unless accompanied in the first place with the mystic rite which is the secret of the Panikkar.

Magic—The Evil Eye.—One day as I reached my camp in the Kôttayam taluk, North Malabar, my ears were assailed by the din of incessant drumming hard by. In the evening I was able to see and converse with the drummer, Châtu by name, aged 23, by caste Malayan. The Malayans are hereditary professional magicians, few in number, inferior in the social scale. They are not the only magicians. We have seen already (Bulletin, Volume III, No. 1, page 50) that some of the Nambûtiri Brahmans practise magic ; but to the Malayan the Nâyar appears as often as to any other kind of mantram-man.

Châtu was delightfully communicative. He had been putting away the effects of the evil eye from one of his cliéntèle ;—hence the din. In effect he said : certain persons have the evil eye by nature. Potta Kannu, blind eye it is called. A person having the evil eye may, while *thinking evil*, infect man, woman or child by simply looking at them. Those who have the evil eye are generally women: men rarely. The cause is in the eye itself. No evil spirit is in any way connected with it. A woman may affect her own child. A person having the evil eye, looking at a beautiful or a healthy child, will affect it without intending to do so. The injury done through the eye is often unintentional. The power of the eye to do mischief is altogether beyond the volition of its possessor; but it is excessively virulent when mischief is really intended. Colour of the eye matters nothing. Nor is possession of the evil eye confined to any caste. He knew a Nambûtiri who had it. The effect of it on a child is that it becomes lean, feverish, loses its well-favoured appearance, and cries in its sleep. Men and women suffer from headaches and pains in the limbs. Animals are disposed to lassitude and eat little. Cows will not give milk.

The Malayaṇ drives away all these unpleasant ailments by invoking an evil spirit Vuḍikandan by name: male, having no wife. By means of magic he *forces* Vuḍikandan to do what he requires of him. But how? The process he would not tell. It is secret. That is, all but the drumming. No one outside the Malayan caste may be initiated into the fearsome mysteries. The spirit Vuḍikandan is used for no other rite. The Malayan also drives out evil spirits.

Châtu presented me with a mantram, a magic verse, written with a style on a cadjan leaf, the common stationery of Malabar, and told me that whenever any part of my person becomes affected by the evil eye, I should whisper the mantram over a piece of string and tie the string round my leg, or other limb or part of the body which suffers, and cure will take place instantaneously.

He works by day: never by night. A whole day is occupied in driving away injury through the evil eye in a bad case. He need not be starving; in fact has a good meal before he begins. The generous Châtu presented me also with a couple of mantrams such as would cure an easy case of harm through the evil eye, and explained their use.

(1) "Ôm: Namo: Bhagavatôm Srîparamêsvaranûm Srî Pârvati yum Pallivêṭa Nâyaṭinnâî Ezhunellumpôl Srî

Pârvati kê kannêru dôsam undâî Srî Paramêsvaran Srî Pârvati ute kannêru dôsem Tîrtâtu pôlê Tîrnupôka Svâmi en guruvînâna."

(I prostrate myself to Bhagavati. When Sri Paramesvaran and Srî Parvati went hunting, Srî Parvati was under the influence of the evil eye; Srî Paramêsvaran then put away this influence. I swear by my guru.)

(2) "Ôm Pêpûti Vôrrûpôti Yerrîkâ Swâhâ Yên Guru Vinâna."

The meaning of this is not clear. "Ôm"=I. "Yerrîka"=burnt. "Swâhâ" (used as a verb)=devour. "Guru Vînâna"=by the guru or teâcher. But in mantrams the word guru invariably means the deity.

Mantram (1) is whispered on sixteen grains of rice: on each grain separately, not on all together. As the mantram is whispered on each grain, the grain is placed in oil. When the sixteen grains have been placed thus in the oil, it is stirred while the mantram (2) is repeated sixteen times. The magician then hands this oil in silence to the person who has been injured by the evil eye. The person receives it also in silence, and rubs it over his head. No word is spoken until he has finished.

Fear of harm from the evil eye is very general. At the corner of the upper story of almost every Nâyar house near a road or path is suspended some object, often a doll-like hideous figure, on which may rest the eye of the passer by. And of course in every field some object is erected for the same purpose.

Magic such as is practised by the Malayan, or the Panikkar, is quite fair and above-board. It is, as a rule, all for good: never for harm. Nearly every misfortune, bodily ill or ailment, and even death is caused by some malignant spirit or through its agency, and the warlock has business everywhere relieving people from their oppression. I feel perfectly safe in saying that every Nâyar believes in magic through and through. No matter what his collegiate course has been, no matter how full of knowledge such as the West can give him, no matter how thrilled he may be by the higher Hinduism which condemns it altogether, he believes in magic as the cause of ills, and he believes in magic for removal of these. It is the last resource always, and the most powerful means in the hands of man. What are medicines, what is all our western science compared to it! The Nâyar will not, I trust, be offended by these remarks, which after all mean nothing more than that he is truly human. Belief in magic and witchcraft, symbolic hurts and cures, and the like, are very deep in human nature ; reason and culture do not efface it. It is one of the earliest heirlooms of the human family, and it will in all probability persist to the end. We cannot think of man as being without it.* Hence the interest in investigating it.

But now, as Patelin's Judge said to the draper, let us return *à nos moutons*. There is nothing secret about the profession of the Panikkar. His rites are secret of course. They are *his* secret. But his profession is an honourable one. He is not ashamed of it, nor will he deny it. That is, so long as he confines his talents to the practice of *good* magic.

With the professor of the more lucrative *black magic*, it is quite another thing. No one will ever admit publicly that he practises *black magic*.

Black magic.—It would never do to avoid altogether the subject of black magic, which is cultivated and practised to a much greater extent in Malabar than elsewhere in the Southern Presidency. I hope to have more to say about it later on when we come to description of some of the lower races, and for the present we must be content with a rather bare description of it. We have seen already that a few Nambûtiri Brahmans practise it. A few Nâyars also do so. But as a rule the man who really works in black magic is the Parayan. The old story. It is always the man of inferior race who is superior in black magic. The Parayans of Malabar are not, I think, identical with the Pariahs (Parayas) of Southern India. There are obvious differences in physique. In parts of rural Malabar one may see a Parayan's little hut far away on the hill side, but one tries in vain to see and speak to its inmates, who flee into the jungle. The Parayans are complete outcastes, and their presence carries pollution to one of any superior caste within about a furlong. It is not too much to say that, as a rule, they are abhorred as the lowest of the low. They eat beef, and are therefore quite outside the pale of Hinduism. I have heard of fairly well authenticated cases of their stealing children of Nâyars, hiding them away in the forest and

* The reader who has not given much attention to the subject of Folklore, may be surprised by the evidence of the persistence of these beliefs in England, available in the publications of the Folklore Society, London. See "County Folklore," chapters on Witchcraft, etc.

bringing them up as their own. The belief that they will steal children helps to some extent to make them dreaded as well as abhorred, but it is as skilled professors of black magic that they are really feared. Ôḍi is the name of the cult, and those who follow it, Parayans as a rule, are able to do many wonderful things. The ordeals to be gone through by the apprentice in the Ôḍi cult are rather trying. Some are so utterly filthy and abominable, eating human excreta being a detail, that even amongst the Parayans, themselves dirty to a degree and accustomed to anything but a high class diet, very few are able to undergo them. Many try, and are unable to proceed. But the man who has gone through them all is a terror. He can make himself invisible, and he can turn himself at will into any animal in order to accomplish his desires. There occurs now and then the death of a woman—a Nâyar or other—enceinte for the first time, the fœtus having been removed for use in black magic.*

The Parayan magician, or Ôḍiyan as he is sometimes called, being a pastmaster in Ôḍi, is credited with power to render himself invisible, using such a fœtus; and even without it, he may force a woman to leave her house at midnight and meet him. There would seem to be some connection, however obscure, with hypnotism and this latter. The Parayan, who turns himself into a bullock, in such guise, circumambulates a house thrice; then, still by means of magic, he compels a certain woman of the household to come out to him. If we follow up popular belief, we find that the Nâyar woman so drawn out of her house is bound to die within three days. But as it is well in a description of this kind, to proceed by illustration when possible, I will quote an authenticated story of a woman having been compelled to leave her house by night. The "walking the dæsil" by the bullock, one of those imaginative performances difficult to account for in human belief, must be left out of the story as no one is said to have seen it.

A Nâyar noticed that, for some days, his wife, who was (contrary to the usual custom, as we have seen it to be) living in his house, appeared to be under some occult influence; and under a premonition that something was

* Not very long ago there was a case of this kind, not far from Palghat, and not only was the fœtus removed but a wisp of straw was substituted in its place; apparently with an idea that, if the space were filled up somehow, the wretched woman would not die!

going to happen he slept across the doorway, so that she could not without waking him leave the house. The door was closed and fastened, he sleeping *inside.* In the early hours of the morning he awoke, and, fearing something unpleasant had taken place as the door was open, he called his brother who was sleeping upstairs. Together they searched for the woman, and found her lying outside in the yard, unconscious. When she recovered her senses, she said that for some nights previous she felt as if she was being called outside, and she tried hard to resist the impulse to go out of the house into the night. At last she could resist no longer and, altogether against her will, unfastened the door and went out. What happened then she knew not. There was neither removal of a fœtus nor death in this case. Such is the story. It is quite possible that stories of the kind are inculcated by wary husbands to keep the women indoors and prevent their being crowned with horns. At any rate the story is one of the kind such as every Nâyar believes. It is, I may say, quite plainly to be seen that, when the Nâyar constructs his house, he takes care that there are certain conveniences, so that the women need never leave the house at night. My narrator was a native gentleman in a position of authority, living at the scene of this strange story when the events related in it occurred not long ago. The persons were named, but I did not question them, as there is much objection to speak of such things to a stranger.

The Ôḍi cult.—The Parayan adepts in the magic Ôḍi cult are to some extent hereditary functionaries.* They form one of those hierarchies, common enough in this country, of which Europeans know so little; of which the people themselves know but little as nothing connected with them or with their system is written. It is custom pure and simple—custom which is the most difficult of all to approach and define within accuracy. We will put down what is known, in the way of popular belief of course, as may be free from error.

Those who belong to it, born into it so to speak, go through a certain novitiate, not easy; but those who wish to join it from outside the fraternity of the cult are required to *prove* themselves worthy to join it; and it is their trials as novices, terrifying and utterly filthy, which

* For much of this which follows I am indebted to Mr. U. Balakrishna Nâyar, who has kindly obtained for me matter which is in a general way, unobtainable to the European.

are truly difficult. Members of the brotherhood are bound to secrecy by solemn oaths, and the secrets of their craft are not allowed lightly to pass to any outsider. A member of the brotherhood may have one or more disciples or apprentices who are in the first place bound to strict obedience. These apprentices fill vacancies in the brotherhood.

He who would be a member of the Ôḍi cult falls at the feet of him whom he would have as master, and begs for initiation into the mysteries. The master tries to dissuade him, but the would-be Ôḍiyan persists; and then, when assent is given, comes the trial. He follows his master to a lonely place by night. The master disappears in mist, and then re-appears as some terrible beast, now standing still, now rushing furiously towards the novice as if to tear him in pieces. If he stands still and unperturbed the novice is considered to have fulfilled *that* test. He is then required to pass the night alone in the forest, which he is made to believe is peopled with strange beings howling horribly. When he has satisfied the master that he is not afraid, he is subjected to other tests, and he is eventually accepted as a novice. He is introduced formally to the brotherhood on a certain selected day, when, having invited them to a feast, pûja is made to the dread spirit worshipped by them—Nîli of Kallaḍikôd or Kallaḍikôd Nîli, as she is called (Kallaḍikôd is the *place* name), through whose aid the Ôḍiyan works his devilment. Flesh and liquor are consumed, and the novice is taught how to procure the magical *Pilla thilum* (infant oil).

The principal ingredient to be used in preparing this is a fœtus of some 6 or 7 months' growth. The Ôḍiyan fixes his eye on some woman, who may be of any caste other than his own, in her first pregnancy. Then, on a selected day, usually a Friday, he proceeds to her house at midnight, provided, that is, he meets with no inauspicious omen on the way. I am not sure what omens are auspicious or the contrary; but at any rate the Ôḍiyan returns home should he meet with an omen which is unfavourable, and starts out again some other night. Transforming himself into a dog, a bullock, a cat or some other quadruped, he walks thrice round the house, shaking vigorously a cocoanut-shell containing *gurusi*, a compound of turmeric water, lime and other substances, the colour of which is red. The woman whose appearance is desired comes out. She cannot help herself. If locked in she bangs her head against the wall, and yells until she is allowed to go out. Once out, she rushes like a mad thing into the arms of the Ôḍiyan. He takes her by the hand and leads her to the courtyard or outside it. At once she is stripped naked. The choru kindi (blood—vessel: the shell) being placed near it, the womb expands, and the fœtus is easily removed in a moment. A few leaves of the mailôsika plant (Polycarpæa spadicea*) are placed as was the other instrument of magic, and the womb contracts to the normal dimensions.

No wonder the Ôḍiyan is feared. By means of this *pilla thilum* he may render himself invisible; in fact he is able to do anything, according to popular belief.

SPIRITS, EVIL AND BENEFICENT, HOW SUBDUED.†

A regular working magician tells us something more of these. The most important of the evil spirits (Dûr murti) are—

Karinkutti.	Bhâiravan.
Kuttichchâttan (we have met him before).	Vanni bhâiravan.
Mâranakutti.	Chotâla bhadra kâli.
Kallâti mûttam.	Dûmapati.
Parakkutti.	Narasihmamûrti.
Ôḍikkutti.	Kâla bhâiravan.
Kuttu bhâiravan.	Ôḍi bhâiravan.

Nearly every man, woman and child in Malabar wears some protective charm against evil spirits. Such charms are also very commonly tied round the necks of cattle, goats and even dogs.

Here follows the recipe for subjection of the spirit Karinkutti into one's service. Of course each spirit is treated always in a totally different way. First you bury a dead black or reddish buffalo. You must not catch your buffalo and kill him. You must find him dead. If you say this is far from easy, I can only remark that the subjection of an evil spirit is not an easy matter. Having buried your buffalo—assuming for the moment that you are a magician, such as the instructions are intended for—you bathe, and while your cloths are wet and clinging to your body, draw the figure chakram, which corresponds to a magic circle, on the ground over the buried buffalo. The

* I am not sure that the correct name is here given for this plant. It may be Alpinia Allughas, the aromatic rhizomes of which are used by natives medicinally.

† For this note, too, I thank Mr. Balakrishna Nâyar.

ground is then plastered over with cowdung. Then you mark out with rice flour an eight-cornered chakram, in the centre of which you place a small piece of cadjan leaf, and you place a similar piece at four corners. You sit with your back to the chakram, facing eastwards in the morning and westwards in the evening while performing pûja. This pûja is, I think, addressed to Karinkutti : not in any way to the sun God who is not then visible. For the pûja you must be supplied with fried grain, beaten rice, rice bran, a fowl, toddy, arrack, some flowers of three colours—one of them the tulsi *(Ocimum sanctum)* —sandalwood-paste, camphor, incense. (Note the use of the sacred tulsi in this diabolical incantation!) While the pûja, which I am unfortunately unable to describe (leaving my directions rather lame) is being performed the mûla mantram of Karinkutti is to be repeated 101 times.

In order to do all this you must bathe 7½ nazhikas (about 2¾ hours) before dawn, and complete the pûja before dawn arrives. But even before this you must stand up to your chest in water and repeat the mûla mantram 101 times. And you must repeat the whole thing *da capo* in the evening. The mantram is thus repeated 404 times in the day. You are not done yet, in fact this is only the beginning. The whole thing is done every day for 21 consecutive days ; and then you will have the evil spirit Karinkutti entirely at your disposal. The person who remains continent, eats but once a day, cooking his own food, may it is said bring the spirit into obedience in less than 21 days.

Subjection of Vanni Bhâiravan is a much more difficult matter, involving much more elaborate ceremonial, details of which may well be spared the reader as the example which has been given is quite adequate.

And the good spirits—

Bhagavati.	Mûkâmi.
Bbadra kâli.	Vîrabhadran.
Hanumân.	Móhini.
Ganapati.	Sarabha Mûrti.
Subrahmanyan.	

The evil and the good spirits are truly a strange collection of beings! Their names help to illustrate what has been said already, that the Hinduism of the west coast is a strange medley of the higher Hinduism with the lower cult of the country. Bhâirava or Kâla Bhâirava (Bhâiravan of the Telugu country) is elsewhere the object of adoration of what is almost a distinct cult, a kind of mixture of Hinduism with Buddhism,—the kâpâlika religion or cult, the novice in which is "taught how to worship Bhaîri dêvam (Kâla Bhâirava) with human blood, by human sacrifice, by drinking liquor from a Brâhman's skull, and by wearing wooden earrings called Kâmâkshi kundala, symbols of the female principle." * The licentious portion of the programme I will leave out, as we can but glance at the Bhâiravan of other parts of Southern India. There, Bhâirava, or by whatever equivalent he may be called, is a male entity; in Malabar, where sex in deities is not of very much moment, Bhâirava is female. Bhadra Kâli, and even Vishnu under another name, is dragged into the category of evil spirits!

The first five of the good spirits are of course, well known. It is odd to find the terrible Bhadra Kâli bracketed with the genial Ganapati and reckoned as a good spirit. Some of the others are local spirits though rated along with emanations of Hinduism.

A point to be noticed here is that the magic which has been described is of that kind which is intimately connected with religion, in that the aid of spiritual beings is sought, and mischief is wrought by their means.

But there is, of course, another side of magic; the sympathetic, which deals in symbolic hurts and cures; of quite another character, being nothing more than a "misdevelopment of natural philosophy."

These divisions of magic, though tolerably distinct, are not therefore always separated. They are sometimes blended.

It was my good fortune, not very long ago, to acquire possession of a couple of grandhas, or palm leaf books, the subject of which is ordinary magic and black magic. Like all works of the kind (these are in the Malayalam character) they are written in such a manner as to be quite unintelligible to the ordinary reader. Letters, symbols, syllables belonging to no known word are employed to express occult meaning. In fact it is more a memorandum than anything else. One of the grandhas is so obscure that translation of it is next to hopeless, for the few who can do so are altogether unwilling to help one to decipher it. The other is composed of Sanscrit and Malayalam words, spelled abominably; but though relatively clear for a book out of a "Mantravâdis" (Warlock's Magicians) library, it, too, contains many blank spaces which can only be filled up by the professional dealer in

* From an article by the writer in the "Journal of the Anthropological Society of Bombay," Vol. I, No. 7, 1889.

magic. Fortunately, by the kindness of Mr. U. Balakrishnan Nâyar, these blanks have been filled up in the translation which he has obtained for me—from *one who knows.*

I will give here an excerpt from it, which is fairly representative of the sympathetic side of magic such as is common in Malabar. It is not, I think, concerned with sympathetic or symbolic magic exclusively, as, unless I am much mistaken, an evil spirit is here also invoked. It is within the domain of black magic, in which, I think, an evil spirit is always made to help if not to work the evil.

It describes how to cause certain pains in the body of another. A mantram is written (here, I think, an evil spirit is called up, though such does not appear to be said), on the stem of the kâitha plant. The stem should be the length of eight fingers. A figure representing the person to be injured is (also) drawn on the stem. A hole is bored to represent the navel. The mantram is repeated, and at each repetition a certain thorn (kâra mollu) is fixed into the limbs of the figure. The name of the person and of the star under which he was born are written on a piece of cadjan leaf, which is stuck into the hole representing the navel. The thorns are stuck in 21 times; that is, removed and replaced 21 times. Two magic circles are drawn below the nipple on the figure. The stem is then hung up in the smoke of the kitchen. A pot of toddy and some other accessories are procured, and with these certain rites are performed by the warlock. When he has concluded them, he moves three steps backwards. He shouts aloud thrice, fixing in again the thorns, thinking all the while of the particular mischief with which he would afflict the person to be injured.

When all this has been done, the person whose figure has been drawn on the stem and pricked with thorns, feels pain as if *he* were being pricked with thorns.

The grandha describes also how an enemy may be stuck dumb. The head of a dark coloured fowl is cut off. The head is then split, and a piece of cadjan on which are written a mantram, the name of the person to be injured, and the name of the star under which he was born, is stuck into the split head which is then sewn up, taking care to stitch the tongue to the beak. The head is then inserted in a certain fruit, which, after being tied up with a withe of a certain creeper nine spans in length, is deposited under the enemy's gateway.

In it, too, we are told how to win over a man, or a quarrelsome husband; how to quiet refractory cows which object to be milked; how to cure a headache; to prevent bad dreams, and so on.

N.B.—A mantram must be spoken, breathed, whispered with extreme accuracy. There must be no omission or false accent. Anything of the kind, or wrong pronunciation, destroys its efficacy at once.

FAMOUS MAGICIANS OF MALABAR.

We will close this chapter on magic which, though painfully inadequate, is already rather too long for its purpose, by mention of some of the famous workers in the art. Those who are familiar with the west coast will at once recall to mind the names of three Brâhman families whose scions are famed throughout the land as possessors of stores of magic, and at the same time—so interwoven is magic with religion!—revered for their saintliness. The eldest member of one of these is said to be "an honoured guest throughout the length and breadth of Kêrala; and on certain State occasions in Trevandrum and elsewhere, his presence is indispensable." A well-known tradition relates how that magic came, so to speak, into the family. (It is not necessary to give the family name, even though it is a household word on the west coast).

Long ago in the days of the Perumals, a Brâhman and his friend were belated in the Yakshi paramba (*yakshi*—female demon, *paramba*—garden) near Trichur.* The place was dreary; nothing but palms around. Suddenly they were accosted by lovely damsels who asked them to pass the night under their roof, and soon they were lodged in a sumptuous house, each in a separate chamber. But in the night, the damsels who had, *Lorelei* fashion, attracted the travellers, resumed their demoniacal forms and ate the Brâhman. His friend they could not touch as he had on his person a grandha sacred to Bhagavati; but in the morning he found himself perched on the top of a palm tree underneath which lay the bones of his friend, the Brâhman.

The Brahman's widow gave birth to a son soon after the strange death of her husband. When the boy was eleven years of age, she related to him how he had been made fatherless. He vowed vengeance on the Yakshis and Gandharvas (male demons) and, like a sensible boy, set about preparation for his life-task. It was not long before he had mastered the Vedas and all learning, and having done so he retired to the jungle, where he was

---

* To this day people avoid this place at night.

engaged in prayer and meditation for seven years. His devotion so pleased Surya, the sun god, that he appeared before him in human form and handed him a grandah, which is to this day the greatest work on magic in existence. The kind attention of the sun god accounts for the prefix "Sûrya" to the family name.

Now well equipped, he made war on the Yakshis and Gandharvas, and compelled the Yakshi who had devoured his father to appear before him. She begged for mercy, offering to serve him faithfully. But he would have none of her and made her enter the sacrificial fire, and she was consumed. Then her Gandharva lover turned up, most inconveniently, and cursed the Brahman magician to suffer death on the forty-first following day. It was now the magician's turn to beg for mercy, and the Gandharva, more merciful than the Brahman had been to the Yakshi, extended it to him. On one condition, however, that on the forty-first day he would worship at the Alangât Tiruvalore temple in expiation. Naturally, he went to fulfil it, and preparatory to worshipping, descended into the temple tank to bathe. All at once he was seized with delirium and raved like a maniac, biting the wooden beams of the bathing shed. He died after enduring frightful agonies. The marks of his teeth are to be seen to this day! Moral—Don't meddle with magic.

Another famous magician was by caste a Ravuthan (a class of Tamil Muhammadans of which there are a few on the west coast) who died about 30 years ago. The story is that having been turned out of his father's house, he was in sad plight, when, awaking from sleep under a tree, a white-bearded Rishi * confronted him and presented him with a grandha of magic, which he put to such good use that he died a very wealthy man. Here are two authenticated stories from the families of Nâyars of good position whom he assisted in each case.

(1) A Nâyar lady, having lost several children in infancy, sought the magician. He came to her house, and asked for a common mud pot, a fowl, some rice and some pepper. With what formality is not said, but the fowl (alive ?), the rice and the pepper were put into the pot, which was buried in the ground under the lady's cot. Every day, she ate some of the rice and pepper, and in due time produced a daughter who is now living.

(2) Nearly every young Nâyar woman wears a talisman, protective against evil spirits. The Ravuthan

---

* It is rather comical, a Rishi appearing to a Muhammadan! Again the queer mixture of religious ideas.

magician was called in to prepare one of these. Placing an ordinary style and a small sheet of copper in a box, he closed it. Presently a noise was heard inside the box; and in a few moments a sound as of the style falling. The box was opened and magic figures were found to be inscribed on the copper sheet. The lady wears the talisman now! The magician must have been in a favourable mood on the occasion, as he is said to have given an additional performance on his own account. When he had placed the style and the tiny sheet of copper in the box, taking two young cocoanuts in his hands, he kept on throwing them in the air and catching them. "What will you have in each?" he asked. "Honey in one and boiled milk in the other" was the answer. Of course these were found in the cocoanuts when they were opened by the magician, but it was somewhat gross of the Nâyar gentleman to test the quality of the milk by turning it into curds the next day. Wonderful stories are told of this man who used to be seen at night carried in a mancheel by invisible bearers, whose weary chant could be heard, but whose bodily presence was beyond the reach of human eye.

The last and the chief of this trio is the once famous Kandeth Nayar who departed this life about a hundred years ago. Every one knows about the Kandeth Nayar, and any one now-a-days who wants to injure another invokes his aid, and resorts to his tomb to fulfil his vow. I understand that sacrifices at his tomb are common, and that his power reaches from the land of shades in almost the same strength as when he lived.

The rather incoherent way in which the terms warlock, magician, have been used seems to demand some explanation. Strictly speaking, the Parayan Ôḍiyan is the only warlock. Magician is scarcely the correct term for the ordinary worker in magic. Nevertheless, it is scarcely possible to avoid a somewhat indiscriminate use of these terms on account of the way in which the functions of the warlock, the magician, the astrologer, and even the priest are really interwoven one with the other. The professed magician is often also the warlock and *vice versâ*. The vernacular word, which is as catholic as that which stands for "Religion," is "mantravâḍi"—mantram man; he who is sought every day of the year by hundreds of the people of Kêrala, to relieve them of their physical troubles and infirmities, to cure their cattle, to injure their enemies, aye, even to destroy them.

APPENDIX A.

The account of the funeral ceremonies which has been given is not, of course, full and accurate as regards all the clans; but it is precise as regards one, and suffices for the present to give a clear idea of the ceremonies as performed by all. There are many interesting features in the ceremonies as performed by the Kiriattil clan. Want of space forbids more than the briefest mention of some of these.

Those who carry the corpse to the pyre are dressed as women, their cloths being wet, and each carries a knife on his person. Two junior male members of the Taravâd thrust pieces of mango wood into the southern end of the burning pyre, and, when they are well lighted, throw them over their shoulders to the southwards without looking round. Close to the northern end of the pyre two small sticks are fixed in the ground, and tied together with a cloth, over which water is poured thrice. All members of the Taravâd prostrate to the ground before the pyre. They follow the Enangru carrying the pot of water round the pyre, and go home without looking round.

They pass to the northern side of the house under an arch made by two men, standing east and west, holding at arms length, and touching at the points, the spade that was used to dig the pit under the pyre, and the axe with which the wood for the pyre was cut or felled.

After this is done the "kodali karma" ceremony, using the spade, the axe and a big knife. These are placed on the leaves where the corpse had lain. Then follows circumambulation and prostration by all; and the leaves are committed to the burning pyre.

APPENDIX B.

At the last moment I have received from Dr. E. Hultzsch, Ph.D., the Government Epigraphist, the following excerpt from the number of the *Epigraphia Indica* which is now under publication, and which with his permission I add to this monograph. It is interesting evidence of the old martial spirit of the Nayars :—

"According to an inscription of the 14th year of his reign (=A.D. 1083–84) the Chola King Kulôttunga I. 'conquered Kuḍamalai-nâḍu, *i.e.*, the Western hill country (Malabar), whose warriors, the ancestors of the Nayars of the present day, perished to the last man in defending their independence.'—*South-Indian Inscriptions*, Vol. III, p. 130.

TRANSLATION OF AN INSCRIPTION OF THE 14TH YEAR OF KULÔTTUNGA I. AT TIRUKKAḺUKKUṈṞAM.

Line 27.—'While all the heroes [1] in the Western hill-country (Kuḍamalai-nâḍu) ascended voluntarily to heaven,' etc.—*South Indian Inscriptions*, Vol. III, p. 147.

---

1 In Malayâlam *châvêr* (Tamil *sâverụ*) means 'one who has elected to die, *moriturus*.'

BIBLIOGRAPHY.

ACHYUTA MENON (C.) The Cochin State Manual. 1911.

ANANTHA KRISHNA AIYAR (L.K.) The Cochin Tribes and Castes. 2 vols. Madras, 1908–12.

BARBOSA (D.) A Description of the Coasts of East Africa and Malabar in the beginning of the 16th century. Translation. Printed for the Hakluyt Society. 1866.

BARTOLOMEO (F.P.S.) A Voyage to the East Indies. Translated from the German. 1800.

BUCHANAN (F.) A Journey from Madras through the Countries of Mysore, Canara and Malabar. 3 vols. 1807.

Census of India, 1901. India: Ethnographic Appendices. 1903.

DAY (F.) The Land of the Perumals, or Cochin, its past and its present. 1863.

GOPALAN NAIR (C.) Malabar Series—Wynad: its peoples and traditions. Madras, 1911.

GOPAL PANIKKAR (T.) Malabar and its Folk. Madras, 1900.

HAMILTON (A.) A New Account of the East Indies. 2 vols. 1744.

INNES (C.A.) Gazetteer of the Malabar and Anjengo Districts. Edited by F.B. Evans. 1908.

LETOURNEAU (Ch.) The Evolution of Marriage and of the Family (Contemporary Science Series).

LOGAN (W.) Malabar. 2 vols. 1887.

NAGAM AIYA (V.) Report on the Census of Travancore, 1891. 1894.

——— The Travancore State Manual. 3 vols. 1906.

RECLUS (É.) Primitive Folk; Studies in Comparative Ethnology (Contemporary Science Series).

Report of the Malabar Marriage Commission. 1891.

SANKARA MENON (M.) The Cochin Census Report, 1901.

STUART (H.A.) Report on the Madras Census, 1891. 1893.

SUBRAHMANYA AIYAR. (N.) The Travancore Census Report, 1901. 1903.

THURSTON (E.) Castes and Tribes of Southern India. 7 vols. Madras, 1909.

——— Ethnographic Notes in Southern India. Madras, 1906.

——— Omens and Superstitions of Southern India. 1912.

VISSCHER (J.C.) Letters from Malabar. Translation. 1862.

WESTERMARCK (E.) The History of Human Marriage. 2nd edn. 1894.

WIGRAM (H.) Malabar Law and Custom. 2nd edn. By L. Moore. Madras, 1900.